GROUNDS FOR BELIEF

IN LIFE AFTER DEATH

George E. Clarkson

Symposium Series
Volume 24

The Edwin Mellen Press
Lewiston/Queenston

Library of Congress Cataloging-in-Publication Data

Clarkson, George E.
  Grounds for belief in life after death.

  Symposium series ; v. 24
  Bibliography: p.
  1. Future life--History of doctrines--20th Century.
  2. Future life--Biblical teaching. I. Title.
  II. Series: Symposium series (Edwin Mellen Press) ;
  v. 24.
  BT904.C63   236'.2   87-24685
  ISBN 0-88946-716-1

> This is volume 24 in the continuing series
> Symposium Series
> Volume 24 ISBN 0-88946-716-1
> SS Series ISBN 0-88946-989-X

Copyright © George E. Clarkson

For information contact:

The Edwin Mellen Press   The Edwin Mellen Press
P.O. Box 450   P.O. Box 67
Lewiston, New York   Queenston, Ontario
USA 14092   CANADA L0S 1L0

Printed in the United States of America

This book is dedicated to my wife, Elizabeth Hutton Clarkson, with thanks for her patience and encouragement over the years that this writing developed.

TABLE OF CONTENTS

Chapter I	Preface	1
Chapter II	Biblical Grounds	3
Chapter III	Nicholas Berdyaev	17
Chapter IV	Gabriel Marcel	35
Chapter V	Paul Tillich	59
Chapter VI	Some Personal Wrestlings	89
Summary		115
Footnotes		117
Selected Bibliography		133
Appendix:		141

Symbols of Eternal Life, The Ingersoll Lecture on the Immortality of Man delivered on February 1, 1962, by Paul Tillich.*

*Reprinted with permission of *The Harvard Divinity Bulletin*, The Harvard Divinity School, Cambridge, Massachusetts

FOREWORD

This treatise grew out of studies at the University of Wales over a five year period. Three of the chapters--one on Marcel, one on Tillich, and one on Berdyaev--were read as papers at meetings of the American Academy of Religion. The last chapter was written in Wales while on a study leave. We lived in a Welsh farmhouse near Pumsaint (Five Saints) in Dyfed County and commuted to St. David's University College in Lampeter as well as to the University of Wales in Aberystwyth. Final revisions were made while I have been on the faculty at Wells College in Aurora, New York.

CHAPTER I
Preface

There is a statement from Oscar Cullman that strikes a good note with us: "An open grave at once reminds us that we are not simply concerned with a matter of academic discussion." (i) When a course is offered in college with the title: "Mind, Body, and Immortality," one quickly realizes that those who enroll, for the most part, are not there just for academic discussion; they are concerned over their own future. The students were exploring their own beliefs, or lack of them, concerning the possibilities of life beyond the event of death. They were concerned not only about what others had thought, but their own encounters with the death of a father or mother or close friend.

The more important matter which concerns us here is the confrontation with the reality of death as it comes to persons near us. I found myself one morning (while working on this very preface) walking away from the house of a friend. In mid-life, he had burned out his life too quickly, and a massive coronary attack had taken him during his sleep. Just the same night (in the evening) when he came home he had talked to me on the phone and made an appointment for us to get together shortly. He had been thoughtful and considerate as we talked and he tried a gentle joke. Now I just watched them take his body away in an ambulance to the morgue and many thoughts went through my head as I walked away. I was thinking mostly of his death and the effect it would have on his family, but I also thought about my own death. One can do no other.

The very "angst," the threat of non-being that we see in Socrates, for example, is also a constant shadow over every one of us. Our humanity is such that none of us knows beyond the moment precisely what lies ahead. "One Day At A Time" is the title of an American TV series, but it may also be the title for each one of us. Perhaps it should be "one moment at a time" for though we all make plans and try to carry them out, each one of us is sure only of the very moment through which he or she is passing.

Sometimes it takes a tragedy or near tragedy to awaken us. One moment we were driving along a quiet road. Then with no warning lights, a huge tractor-trailer moved off the shoulder and quickly went across the entire road. We braked but ended striking a beam under the trailer. A sturdy car and safety belts held. The car was damaged but we were unhurt. But one does not shake this off easily. Others in similar encounters ended in death. But we were, for that moment, on the brink. Every day, encounters with death push us to think seriously. Is there anything beyond death, and if so, how can we be sure? We will sort out some thinking, turning first to some biblical sources, then to three thinkers (among many) who have helped me. And then we will attempt a personal affirmation that has come out of serious wrestling with this weighty problem.

CHAPTER II
Biblical Grounds

There is a wealth in biblical literature. But as we look at them, it becomes quite clear that only glimmers of hope are found in the Old Testament. <u>The resurrection ideas grew up largely in the intertestamental period and took new and decisive form in the era surrounding Jesus and the early church.</u> Some Christian ideas are often, in our day, read back into Old Testament passages, but the concept of resurrection had only embryonic beginnings there. Elements of hope are present but not with reference to resurrection. In Job and some of the Psalms we can find elements of hope but that is as far as we see them develop.

We see this in Job in a passage such as this one:

> If a tree is cut down,
> there is hope that it will sprout again
> and fresh shoots will not fail.
> Though its roots grow old in the earth,
> and its stump is dying in the ground,
> if it scents water it may break into bud
> and make new growth like a young plant.
> But if a man dies, and he disappears;
> man comes to his end, and where is he?
> As the waters of a lake dwindle,
> or as a river shrinks and runs dry,
> so mortal man lies down, never to rise
> until the very sky splits open.
> If a man dies, can he live again?
> He shall never be roused from his sleep.
> If only thou wouldst hide me in Sheol
> and conceal me till thy anger turns aside,
> if thou wouldst fix a limit for my time there,
> and then remember me!
> Then I would not lose hope, however long my service,

> waiting for my relief to come.
> Thou shouldst summon me, and I would answer thee;
> thou wouldst long to see the creature thou hast
> made. (i)

This time, it seems that we can discover some words of hope, some honest expectations. Job is grasping, seeking to explore the possibilities of God who cares. Even though that God has caused him to suffer, he still is convinced that in the long run, God will restore him, will want to see him as he was created. Perhaps then, he is saying, there is some possibility that Sheol is not the end, but a place where I would be held awaiting the day of God's choosing. He does not use a word for resurrection and does not speak of it that way. It is rather a restoration that he hopes for, that he will be restored in God's favour and that he will once again have some form of life. No matter who the author of the book of Job may be, that author has Job struggling not only with the problem of evil and suffering but with some dim hopes that are hidden deep within and now are giving expression.

The struggle continues much later in the play as Job gives vent to a more typical view of Sheol and uses the word of perdition: "Abaddon."

> In the underworld the shades writhe in fear,
> the waters and all that lives in them are struck
> with terror.
> Sheol is laid bare,
> and Abaddon uncovered before him. (ii)

But there is still some dim hope, as he expresses the idea of being held by God from going over the edge of the pit.

> ...God makes them listen,
> and his correction strikes them with terror.
> To turn a man from reckless conduct,
> to check the pride of mortal man,
> at the edge of the pit he holds him back alive
> and stops him from crossing the river of death. (iii)

This same idea is re-echoed a few lines later, that is, the idea of being saved from going over the edge of the pit, but then he proceeds once more to speak of the possibility (that few others in the Old Testament seem to see) of being brought back again from that pit and finding life once more. There is some hope again. But part of this indicates that it may be man who saves himself, not the spirit of God.

>...then he saves himself from going down to the pit,
>he lives and sees the light.
>All these things God may do to a man,
>again and yet again,
>bringing him back from the pit
>to enjoy the full light of life. (iv)

We have tried to avoid reading too much into the Job saga but there are some groupings there, some glimmers there, some dim hope. And this we must recognize for it has a unique role among Old Testament documents. Part of Job's struggle with suffering and misfortune also involves him in a struggle of faith where he wonders seriously about the world beyond. It is not only a literary masterpiece but an utterly human document and even centuries later some of us can identify with the spiritual wrestlings of this man.

One other area of literature in the Old Testament that gives us some important views on life after death is the collection of Psalms. Once again, dating is difficult and must be varied. Generally, we would say that they would represent a later viewpoint, but it is as varied as the Psalms are with use of a number of the Hebrew words for a life after death, some with little hope in mind, some with strains of clear groping and perhaps even a grasp of a hopeful idea. And it is also clear that the grounds for hope of life after death in the book of Psalms are those which we found, even dimly, in Job--namely a confidence in the goodness of God. It is a belief in God that is at the root of this confidence.

There were some six or seven different words used in the Old Testament for the world of life after death. In several references it is "the Ditch," "the Pit," the "realm of Wealth," the "nethermost earth" (sometimes "earth"), "perdition," and perhaps most often: "Sheol." The trust is that none of these phrases in themselves hold the hope and joy that we in the Christian tradition are convinced should be there. Sheol becomes more a spirit world where everyone's spirit merges with all other spirits. We do not think in early Hebraic thought forms but are affected both by Christian concepts and some persistent soul/body ideas that are not in the Old Testament.

We do find some hopeful Psalms and we find them used to-day at funerals and memorial services. We find the 90th Psalm assuring us:

> Lord, thou has been our dwelling place in all generations. Before the mountains were brought forth, or ever thou hast formed the earth and the world, even from everlasting to everlasting, thou art God. (v)

The 121st Psalm asserts that "The Lord shall preserve thy going out and thy coming in from this time forth, and even for evermore." (vi) And over and over we think of the richness of the 23rd Psalm: "Yea, thou I walk through the valley of the shadow of death, I will fear no evil; for thou art with me; thy rod and thy staff they comfort me." (vii) And we have often found hope as we read from the 139th Psalm:

> If I ascend to heaven, thou art there!
> If I make my bed in Sheol, thou art there!
> If I take the wings of the morning and dwell
>   in the uttermost parts of the sea,
> Even there thy hand shall lead me,
>   and thy right hand shall hold me. (viii)

There are assurances but ideas about resurrection and eternal life are yet to come--centuries later--in the Christian era.

Later Christian writers who wrote about resurrection did not draw from these Old Testament documents for the most part but drew rather from ideas that grew up in what we regard as the intertestamental period. Strong positions about punishment and reward grew up in this period and images of a world of punishment and reward after death also were developing. The positions of the major religious parties in Jesus' day illustrate this growth of ideas. The Sadducees represent the more traditional Jewish viewpoint (of the "Old Testament") while the Pharisees did believe in a resurrection. So, when Jesus talked about resurrection, or when His followers interpreted the events following his death in this light, they were not writing in a vacuum but were drawing upon ideas already developing. They were drawing from a vast array of writings, so complex that it still baffles some of our finest scholars. For us, the important thing to note is that this development did take place before New Testament times. It seems very difficult to understand why references to this period are nonexistent in many contemporary works on life after death.

It is clear that by the first and second centuries B.C. strong ideas about life after death had emerged and become an important part of Jewish thinking. Walter Eichrodt expresses this well:

> From the second century onwards evidences multiply that <u>the concept of eternity has been accepted into the community's life of faith</u>. Even though it was never able to enjoy universal recognition, it was still felt by the religiously most vital section of the community to be the indispensable final note in their assurance of salvation, and gave their faith an even greater sense of superiority to the religious thinking of heathenism. The passion with which it is used in II Maccabees in controversy with the heathen oppressors shows how men's sense of the unconditional character of God's demand is now linked indissolubly with the assurance of

eternal election or rejection even for the individual. (ix)

The Hebraic emphasis continued strong and meant that there was a persistence of the view of one as a whole person, and a strong concern over <u>this</u> world, not another. Even as resurrection ideas appear, they tended to think of a "total" resurrection, that is of the whole person including a body.

S.H. Hooke in his 1967 volume on "The Resurrection of Christ as History and Experience" underlines some of the special direction that Hebrew thought followed in the development of views on resurrection.

> ...the idea of resurrection as distinct from the idea of survival after death had a special development in the religious thought of Israel, and the stage which that development had reached in the time of Jesus forms the background and setting in the light of which we may understand the state of mind of the disciples upon whom the resurrection of Christ burst with such startling effect. Moreover, the development of the idea of Israel cannot be considered in isolation. From the earliest period of its history as a people Israel was exposed to the various currents of thought at work in the religious history of the nations by whom she was surrounded. (x)

In brief summary fashion we could see the beginnings of a belief in resurrection having its roots that included several factors.

1. As with other ideas about life after death, it is a part of a human search for hope beyond the event of death. There was a time in Hebrew history when this hope was a hope of living on as a part of a community. In early thought it was not centered upon the individual. In other words, just being human included a hope for an existence beyond death.

2. Some of the beliefs arose from the ashes of exile, but of the despair of being conquered and taken from their homeland. Out of this came some hopes with seers such as Daniel envisioning the strong possibility of their nation rising up again. This was a kind of corporate resurrection idea. The nation will rise again.

3. In its development, the resurrection idea has roots in a Judaic view of persons, not a Platonic view of dualistic nature. Resurrection was thought of, for some, as a resurrection of the total person. This was also part of the development of a concept of a "spiritual body."

4. Ideas of punishment and reward grew up and added to the hopes about life after death. This was probably due to a strong sense of justice and injustice; if you did not have your reward here, then a good God would reward you in a life after death.

5. The rise of a sense of the importance of the individual also added some new dimensions and moved the development of the concept from a communal concept to one that saw the individual having an identifiable future beyond death.

George W.E. Nickelsburg, Jr. comments on an intertestamental work that has a Hellenistic influence to show the direction of thought as developed in that work:

> It is commonly observed that the Wisdom of Solomon teaches immortality of the soul rather than resurrection of the body...Regardless of what happens to the bodies of the righteous, their souls are in God's hand and cannot be touched by torment. Different from Daniel 12 and the Testament of Judah 25, here judgment after death does not require a resurrection of the body because, in spite of the destruction of the body, the soul continues to exist and can be judged. (xi)

A book in the Apocrypha that has strong ideas about immortality is the Wisdom of Solomon. Though the word and some of the concepts are borrowed from Hellenism, the word "immortality" in the Wisdom of Solomon carries strong Jewish ideas along with it. Professor Clarke is quite insistent that "immortality is not the immortality of the soul in the Greek sense of the pre-existence of the soul.... The writer's view that personality resided in the soul (8:19-20) was a logical extension of the Hebrew ideas on life after death...the word 'immortal' is never used with the idea of life/soul in Wisdom." (xii) "In Hebrew thought the tendency was to connect personality with the body while Greek philosophy favoured associating personality with the soul. The writer of Wisdom has taken a tentative step in the direction of Greek thinking while at the same time rejecting an either/or conclusion." (xiii)

Quite in contrast to the views expressed at the beginning of the book, there are many passages that have the ring of the certainty of immortality, either as the way God rewards the virtuous or as the way in which one is remembered. "It is better to be childless, provided one is virtuous; for virtue held in remembrance is a kind of immortality because it wins recognition from God, and from men too." (xiv) Since God is a judge, and since virtue is to be rewarded, ideas of punishment and reward are found in this work. Certainly some of this reward is in this life. "In the moment of God's coming to them they will kindle into flame, like sparks that sweep through stubble; they will be judges and rulers over the nations of the world, and the Lord shall be their king for ever and ever." (xv)

It is R.H. Charles who comments that the doctrine of the resurrection "was made a commonplace of Jewish theology by I Enoch." (xvi) Retribution ideas developed at this time but they differed from some in earlier Hebrew writings as in Ezekiel. And there is some identification of Sheol with hell. The religious parties of Sadducees and Pharisees had evolved by this time and in I Enoch one sees discussions relating to the Sadducees' position upholding an older and more orthodox view. There are also here some soaring passages that could be much like those of earlier prophets. There is hope here and words of encouragement and praise to those who have followed the Lord and obeyed his percepts. The separation between sinners and the elect is quite clear and often reoccurs.

> And in those days shall the mountains leap like
> rams
> And the hills also shall skip like lambs satisfied
> with milk,
> And the faces of the angels in heaven shall be
> lighted up with joy.
> And the earth shall rejoice,
> And the righteous shall dwell upon it,
> And the elect shall walk thereon. (xvii)

The picture of the New Jerusalem and the resurrection of the righteous continues as the writer brings in the figure of the sheep and weaves a vision into words. There are many elements in the vision: the threat and certainty of judgment, the promise of a dwelling for those who are faithful, whiteness, purity and hope--all mingled as elements of the new life.

In the work "Of the Secrets of Enoch," one finds descriptions of paradise for the righteous. It is interesting to trace these ideas for here one may catch glimpses of thought present in Jewish writings at the time of the beginning of the Christian community. Certainly there is much here not found in Old Testament writings. Look at this passage as an example:

> And paradise is between corruptibility and incorrupt-
> ibility...And two springs come out which send forth
> honey and milk, and their springs send forth oil
> and wine, and they separate into four parts, and
> go round with quiet course, and go down into the
> paradise of Eden, between corruptibility and incor-
> ruptibility. And hence they go forth along the
> earth, and have a revolution to their circle even
> as other elements. And here there is no unfruitful

> tree, and every place is blessed. And there are three hundred angels very bright, who keep the garden, and with incessant sweet singing and never-silent voices serve the Lord throughout all days and hours. And I said, 'How very sweet is this place,' and those men said to me: 'The showing to Enoch of the place of the righteous and compassionate. This place, O Enoch, is prepared for the righteous...who avert their eyes from iniquity, and...give bread to the hungering...raise up the fallen, and help injured orphans, and who talk without fault before the face of the Lord, and serve him.' (xviii)

In this very sketchy survey of some of the intertestamental literature, we are obviously not attempting either to make significant new contributions to scholarship of that period nor are we attempting to be complete. Many others have written worthy works to which one could turn. What we are suggesting here in a brief chapter is that the growth of resurrection ideas did take place during this crucial period and must be considered if we wish at all to see the origins of some of these life-after-death ideas we see in Christianity. II Baruch was a polemical document opposed in many ways to positions of the early church. Yet the early church preserved it and gave it circulation. In it we can see resurrection ideas developed quite fully. In fact they have developed so far that Charles points out that "the Pauline teaching in I. Cor. xv. 35-50 is in many respects not an innovation, but a developed and more spiritual expression of ideas already current in Judaism." (xix)

What we have seen to this point is that ideas about resurrection did develop strongly during the intertestamental period. We wrote earlier in this chapter about the development of the Sadducees and Pharisees as religious parties. The whole development of these points of view came about through this period of writing that we have been summarizing briefly. When the New Testament writers wrote about resurrection ideas, they were not creating them, nor developing a new idea but were building on the development through centuries of Jewish thought prior to their time. And when they spoke of resurrection with respect to Jesus, it was not surprising but rather only a matter of how to describe what was happening in the light of belief in resurrection ideas.

Along with this development, we have also seen a growth in concepts of heaven and hell, of reward and punishment. These too were carried into the life and writings of the New Testament times. Some of the more commonly held views about heaven and hell are not to be found explicitly in the New Testament but actually were developed later during the Middle Ages.

Baruch writes that:

> ...the first shall rejoice and the last shall not be grieved. For they know that the time has come of which it is said, that it is the consummation of the times. But the souls of the wicked, when they behold all these things, shall then waste away the more. For they shall know that their torment has come and their perdition has arrived. (xx)

The key passages in II Baruch are found in chapters 49 and 50 and become the base on which one could build a comparison between these ideas and some that are found in Pauline thought. In a note in this edition of the Pseudepigrapha Charles once again speaks of this connection indicating that he sees Paul's thought as derivative, not as clearly original. "Paul was not altogether an innovator, but an able and advanced expositor of some current Jewish ideas." (xxi) This following passage then could shed some important light on ideas about the resurrection body and the way it should appear. It has strength and clarity, even with its flowing language that, in many ways, is not far from the more well-known passage from the apostle

Paul. It takes the form of a prophetic dialogue between Baruch and God.

> Nevertheless, I will again ask from Thee, O Mighty One, yea, I will ask mercy from Him who made all things. 'In what shape will those love who live in Thy day? Or how will the splendour of those who (are) after that time continue? Will they then resume this form of the present, and put on these entrammelling members, which are not involved in evils, and in which evils are consummated, or wilt Thou perchance change these things which have been in the world as also the world?' And He answered and said unto me: 'Hear, Baruch, this word, and write in the remembrance of thy heart that thou shalt learn. For the earth shall then assuredly restore the dead...It shall make no change in their form, but as it has received, so shall it restore them, and as I delivered them unto it, so also shall it raise them.' (xxii)

New Testament ideas also compose such a vast body that we can only comment in a cursory way here. Again, we are not trying to duplicate what so many others have done with competence. There are rich new affirmations in the New Testament, particularly in the Gospel of John and Paul's letters. Some of these ideas will come to the fore in later chapters and with strength in our last chapter. Though this is just a rapid survey, we wanted to show where some resurrection ideas developed. And when Jesus was pushed for an answer from Sadducees who represented the "old-time religion" views of Sheol, Jesus was found on the side of the Pharisees who did believe in resurrection. We now turn to some twentieth-century writers to see the insights they may add to our search.

We shall look at three major thinkers to see their views on life after death, on eternal life. Each writer has important viewpoints in many works. Tillich was one of a distinguished line of thinkers to give an Ingersoll lecture on immortality at Harvard. Marcel's views are partly in a lecture as part of the Gifford lectures in Scotland. Berdyaev's views are well compressed in the ending of a major book. Though many thinkers have added dimensions to our thinking, these three have very special contributions to make.

In any survey of writers such as we are attempting, we will find different viewpoints expressed but in some areas there is a kind of unanimity that is important. Each rejects a conception of life after death that is heavily judgmental. It is true that an element of judgment rests upon our lives constantly and this cannot be avoided as one faces death. But, for these writers, life after death is not a time of reward and punishment. It represents, on the other hand, the probability of an ongoing quality of living that brings hope. Especially in this area of concern where empirical evidence is difficult to obtain, our hope does not have to rely literally on putting our hands into the wounds. Our hope may and should rest in words of assurance from the Christ in whom we believe, and from confidence in intuitional knowledge out of which come beliefs in our own nature and the nature of the God of love who blesses us.

CHAPTER III
Nicholas Berdyaev

Certain principles are so central in the thinking of Nicolas Berdyaev that we must look at these tenets to understand the basis for his thinking on eternal life. Though he does stand in the existentialist tradition, he is quite different even from other twentieth-century religious existentialists. One of the reasons for this is his background as a Russian Orthodox and the other reason might be found in the thinkers who seriously affected him. One of these influences may be found in Jacob Boehme who also heavily influenced aspects of Paul Tillich's thought. But the two thinkers, Tillich and Berdyaev, move in quite different directions though they were aware of each other's positions. Boehme's influence is considerably more evident in Berdyaev than in Tillich though both write about Boehme many times.

This influence is particularly evident in the concept of the Ungrund and its relationship to our thinking about God, freedom, the nature of persons and the source of evil. This is a very important starting point for Berdyaev, and we must deal with it even though briefly. This influence came from Boehme but other writers also affected him, particularly Pushkin, Tolstoi and Dostoyevsky. From Dostoyevsky he also found strong strains about freedom. Fuad Nucho points out that some of Berdyaev's attitude towards and interest in freedom may well have come from his Russian Orthodox background.

> The Orthodox Church experienced no Reformation and Counter-Reformation and, consequently, escaped the necessity of redefining and overdefining its theological terms and recasting its dogmas in rigid doctrinal forms. This means that there is more theological elbow-room in Orthodoxy than is the case in Protestantism or Catholicism. It means a greater measure of freedom of thought. For Berdyaev, these qualities were highly significant. (i)

Life is such a unique one that one could spend many pages on it (which we will not do). Mlle. Davy has written a very able volume in this regard with sections on his thought. (ii) She knew him well and could write from the inside of the intellectual groups in Paris that Berdyaev fostered. His own autobiography ("Dream and Reality") though out of print is most helpful in this regard. He does not speak, as Tillich does in "Courage To Be" for example, of the angst of death, but its finality does drive thoughts home. "I am not prone to the fear of death, as, for instance, Tolstoi was, but I have felt intense pain at the thought of death and a burning desire to restore to life all who have died." (iii) His account of the death of his son, and then shortly afterwards his wife whom he loved greatly, indicates that death was not an abstract matter to be dealt with objectively.

The writings that were valid during all of his life came from a period when as a young man Berdyaev held rather radical political views and was enamoured of Marxism. Some of the first parts of "The Meaning of The Creative Act" were written as early as 1910 and it was completed in 1914 (revised somewhat in 1927). "The Destiny of Man," which he regarded as central to himself, came to him in part as a plan of writing rather suddenly while watching a Diaghilev ballet in 1912 though it first appeared in English translation in 1935. Mlle. Davy says that Berdyaev never had totalitarian leanings but was always one who espoused ideas about freedom. He reacted strongly to his aristocratic upbringing (though he was later grateful that he was reared in a home where French was spoken), and even as a member of the Soviet in the time of the revolution, he spoke clearly of his views that brought his arrests and finally expulsion from the country he always loved. He spent all his remaining years in Paris.

A clear starting point for Berdyaev is in his view of Spirit. Insofar as we participate in freedom, we are in the world of spirit. "Spirit is not a principle," he says, "but personality, in other words the highest form." (iv) Here Berdyaev is saying that that which lives eternally is our spirit self. His views on life after death are heavily found in Part III of his work "The Destiny of Man." We will find creative views on Heaven, Hell and Eternal Life.

Just as Wordsworth writes of "Intimations of Immortality..." so Berdyaev says that all have many intimations of the meaning of death though one cannot know the full meaning of one's own death until it comes upon us. Death involves a final parting, and Berdyaev says that all of life involves a sequence of partings.

> Death is an event embracing the whole of life. Our existence is full of death and dying. Life is perpetual dying, experiencing the end in everything, a continual judgment passed by eternity upon time....When, in space, we part with a person, a house, a town, a garden, an animal, and have the feeling that we may never see them again, this is an experience of death. The anguish of every parting, of every severance in time and space, is the experience of death. (v)

In his Ingersoll lecture (1942), Douglas Steere speaks of similar experiences in life as the "little deaths." (vi) But both may be quite right in assuming that these experiences of deaths and partings may be the clearest intimations about the meaning of the final death that we have.

Berdyaev has a strong Christocentric theology and sees in the person of Christ the Redeemer who not only liberates us from the world of suffering (vii) but also who brings eternal life to us. The Resurrection, he says, is a "cosmic miracle" in which "meaning has triumphed over meaninglessness." (viii) Hence, he sees this approach in opposition to the idea of "natural immortality" for that stance does not presuppose a struggle and one does not just inherit immortality or eternal life. The doctrine of the resurrection, for him, "presupposes the struggle of spiritual forces with the powers of death. Resurrection means spiritual victory over death, it leaves nothing to death and corruption, as abstract spiritualism does. The doctrine of resurrection recognizes the tragic fact of death and means victory over it." (ix) This view, he continues, ties our destiny with world-destiny. "The resurrection of my body is at the same time the resurrection of the body of the world. 'Body' in this connection means of course 'spiritual body' and not the material frame. A complete personality is connected with the body and the eternal form of it and not merely with the soul." (x) Our participation in eternal life, then, according to Berdyaev, is not by virtue of some eternal, immortal nature but through the resurrection of the spiritual body, in a Pauline sense, made possible by the Resurrection of the Christ. "If it had not been for the coming of Christ and His Resurrection, death would have triumphed in the world and in man." (xi)

For the most part, Berdyaev, as with some other thinkers, shows a strong preference for the word "eternal" rather than "immortality." The two words in Berdyaev's writings may be synonymous at times though he may have intended some distinctions. It is in one such place where these words are used together that he does make it clear how eternal life may be spoken of objectively even though he usually opposes objectification.

> The paradox of time and eternity exists for the destiny both of the world and of the individual. Eternal and immortal life may be objectified and naturalised, and then it is spoken of as life in the world beyond. It appears as a natural realm of being though different from ours. Man enters it after death. But eternal and immortal life regarded from within and not objectified is essentially different in quality from the natural and even the supernatural existence. It is a spiritual life, in which eternity is attained while still in time....Eternal life is revealed in time, it may unfold itself in every instant as an eternal present. (xii)

It is also clear that though the eternal may be revealed in the present that it is not a life "in the future." If it is present in this life, it is present in the depths, so he says. Here Berdyaev uses one of the same descriptive words we find in Tillich--in the depth.

> It is therefore a mistake to expect eternity in the future, in an existence beyond the grave and to look forward to death in time in order to enter in to the divine eternal life. Strictly speaking, eternity will never come in the future--in the future there can only be a bad infinity. Only hell can be thought of in this way. (xiii)

So when we experience eternal life, it does not come in the future, but in a moment, in a possibility that is delivered from time itself.

It is no doubt a reflection on the mood of the twentieth-century religious thought that there are so few references (in the writers with whom we are dealing) to hell. But when we read Berdyaev we find him writing at some length about this. And this is in spite of his strong remarks about sadistic movements within religious groups including Christianity. In his Part III of the "Destiny of Man," he has an entire chapter on hell and has another one largely on it in "Truth and Revelation." (xiv) And in both he has a strong relationship to a discussion of ethics. His very opening words in the "Destiny of Man" chapter on hell reads thus: "Philosophical ethics has left untouched the problem of hell, which existed for religious ethics only. And yet hell is not only the final but the fundamental problem of ethics and no thoroughgoing system of ethics can dispense with it." (xv) He sees our easy skirting of the subject as a "most striking evidence of human frivolity." It is because we live "on the surface and then the image of hell does not haunt." (xvi)

This may seem like an extreme position until we see his full view of hell and its relationship to the concept of freedom for example. It soon becomes clear that if freedom is genuine, then we have a full right to choose either extreme or somewhere in the middle. The fact that there must be an extreme to make full choices genuine is part of the reason that Berdyaev sees a concept of hell as important as it now seems to be. We may condense some of his argument in this wise:

> It is easy enough to deny hell if one denies freedom and personality. There is no hell if personality is not eternal and if man is not free, but can be forced to be good and to enter paradise. The idea of hell is ontologically connected with freedom and personality, and not with justice and retribution...In a certain sense man has a moral right to hell--the right freely to prefer hell to heaven....It is the idea of freedom and not of justice that dialectically presupposes hell. Hell is admissible in the sense that a man may want it and prefer it to paradise; he may feel better there than in heaven. (xvii)

In "Truth and Revelation" Berdyaev again emphasizes this relationship of freedom to evil as well as to good. "But freedom assumes the experience of evil. Compulsory good, good imposed by force, would be the very greatest of evils. Dostoyevsky showed that he understood this better than anyone in the way he describes the Utopias which are to bring paradise on earth in the dialectic of 'The Grand Inquisitor.'" (xviii)

Berdyaev does not waste words in defining what he means by hell or perdition. "Eternal perdition means that personality remains self-contained, indissoluble and absolutely isolated. Hell consists precisely in the fact that the self does not want to give it up." (xix) "Hell is not eternity at all but endless duration in time." (xx) This is a persistent emphasis. Hell is bound up with the world of time, endlessly, whereas eternity has brought deliverance from this plight. Berdyaev is not trading the idea of hell historically but is using the word in his own way. But he has a bit of satire that is delightful in a way for he indicates that if some common ideas of hell (and sinners) held by some in some branches of the church are true then he would not want to live in paradise!

> Paradise is impossible for me if the people I love, my friends or relatives or mere acquaintances, will be in hell--if Boehme is in hell as a 'heretic,' Nietzsche as 'an antichrist,' Goethe as a 'pagan,' and Pushkin as a sinner. Roman Catholics who cannot take a step in their theology with Aristotle are ready to admit with perfect complacency that, not being a Christian, Aristotle is burning in hell. All this kind of thing has become impossible for us, and that is a tremendous moral progress. If I owe so much to Aristotle or Nietzsche I must share their fate... (xxi)

Hell has another dimension, if we may call it that. It is a state of separation from the ability to love and is also a separation from God as well. Hell means a separation "from everyone and from everything, completely isolated and at the same time enslaved by everything and everyone." (xxii) It becomes evident that hell is not a place, neither is it a state wherein God wreaks his vengeance upon those who are there. "Hell is nothing other than complete separation from God... It is not what God will do to me that is terrible, but what I will do to myself.... Hell really means not that man falls into the hands of God but that he is finally abandoned to his own devices." (xxiii) Hell as a state of self-centeredness is also then a state of one incapable of loving; "the moment becomes endless time." Berdyaev adds later in the paragraph that "religious belief consists in the very fact that this hell will not be eternal." (xxiv) In "Destiny of Man" nearly the same words are found: "hell will not come in eternity, it will remain in time. Hence it cannot be eternal." (xxv)

This concept does raise a problem that perhaps cannot be solved. Or it may mean that, if this view is consistently held eventually all persons will have the chance to enter paradise since only paradise is eternal. If one is in hell and therefore is still in time, is it possible that this dimension of time might end? "Only those are in hell who have not entered eternity but have remained in time. It is impossible, however, to remain in time forever: one can only remain in time for a time." (xxvi) Berdyaev also adds his view that to think of being eternally damned for some act that was quickly and perhaps precipitously done is unthinkable. "There is something hideous and morally revolting in the idea of eternal torments as a just retribution for the crimes and sins of a short moment of life. Eternal damnation as the result of things done in a short period of time is one of the most disgusting of human nightmares." (xxvii)

One further matter should be discussed though we are far from relaying the many historical references that Berdyaev uses to illustrate his positions. He also relates his views on hell to the idea of meonic freedom and non-being, an idea that he took substantially from Boehme. And he ties this up with a Christocentric theology once more. The realm of hell is not that of reality but that of "non-being, the realm of dark meonic freedom, the illusory subjective realm." (xxviii) Now it is the self-centered world that is illusory. (One must say in corrective that there is also a genuine subjective world where one is not self-centered but one has a relationship to others in love.) Since these forces of evil are meonic (non-being) in roots according to Berdyaev, this is a limitation on God who cannot control them in their sources. He says "victory over meonic freedom is impossible for God" but he cannot fully mean this for he denies it only a few sentences later. If the victory does come from Christ, Christ's power comes from His oneness with the Father. Hence the victory that Berdyaev sees possible does come from God. He probably would continue to insist that God does not control meonic forces in their source, but he denies his bold sentence in a passage that follows. After writing of the impossibility of God's victory over meonic freedom, he also insists that this is

> ...equally impossible for man, since man has become the slave of that dark freedom and is not free in his freedom. It is possible only for the God-man Christ Who descends into the abysmal darkness of meonic freedom, and in Whom there is perfect union and interaction between the human and the Divine. Christ alone can conquer the horror of hell as a manifestation of the creature's freedom... The salvation from hell is open to all in Christ the Saviour. (xxix)

It is quite clear in several statements from Berdyaev that he does believe in a kind of universal salvation: he who knows the Christ must help those who do not know the saving power to find a way to a victory over hell and evil, to live eternally. He at one point blames the Emperor Justinian for some of the insistence on eternal torments for the wicked. So, Berdyaev cites Justinian's condemnation of Origen for this doctrine about universal salvation. "Justinian was not content with there being temporal torments in this world, he wanted eternal torments in the next. It is time we stopped following the Emperor Justinian, but went against him. Let 'the good' no longer interfere with saving the 'wicked' from hell." (xxx)

The final word that he may have to say about hell is partly a preface to what he says about "paradise" for hell is not the victor. It is only a descriptive term for a world of those who are not possessed by eternal life. In his concluding passage in "Destiny of Man" on this subject, he reverses what he says two pages earlier about victory over meonic freedom being impossible for God. One has to assume that what he means, as we hinted, in the earlier passage is that God is not in control over the source of meonic freedom. But he does come to this strong message:

> The problem of hell is an ultimate mystery that cannot be rationalised.... We cannot and must not

> construct any rationalistic doctrine of hell, whether
> optimistic and pessimistic. But we can and must
> believe that the power of hell has been vanquished
> by Christ, and that the final word belongs to God
> and to the Divine meaning. The conception of hell
> deals not with the ultimate but with the penultimate
> realities. (xxxi)

When we turn to the other side of the discussion, we may reverse some things that Berdyaev says about hell and see that they describe aspects of paradise. This is true of the element of time. Hell is endless time, endless duration as Berdyaev sees it. Eternity does not have either past or future. In "Solitude and Society" Berdyaev shows how eternity and the inner life adds a new dimension to time. "The inner life is not governed by numerical time. The intensity of the inner life modifies the nature of time and endows it with a new dimension." (xxxii) From this he sees some intimations about changes in the dimension of time that may indicate the timeless world of eternity. "Everyone knows how time accelerates or slows down according to the intensity of life and the nature of the events that make up human existence....Creative inspiration can likewise dispense with numerical time." (xxxiii) But eternity itself is beyond and qualitatively different from the world of time. "The idea of eternity is opposed to the nightmare of both finite and infinite time." (xxxiv) He is clearly not talking about the future life (which would be an extension of the world of time) but about eternal life.

> ...paradise is not in the future, is not in time,
> but in eternity. Eternity is attained in the actual
> moment, it comes in the present--not in the present
> which is a part of the broken up time, but in the
> present which is an escape from time. Eternity
> is not a cessation of movement and of creative
> life; it is creative life of a different order,
> it is movement which is not spatial and temporal
> but inward... (xxxv)

Persons when discussing some ideas about life after death often come out with the expression--"Well, no one knows about it for no one has been there and returned." Berdyaev does not pose to have been there and come back, but he sees some clear hints or intimations as to what paradise might be like. There is a "foretaste" he says "given us in ecstasy." In such a moment time seems to stand still.

> ...time, as we know it, is rent asunder, the distinction between good and evil disappears, all sense of heaviness is gone and there is a feeling of final liberation. The ecstasy of creative inspiration, of love, of contemplating the divine light, transfers us for a moment to heaven, and those moments are no longer in time. But after a moment of eternity we find ourselves in the continuing time once more; everything grows heavy, sinks down and falls prey to the cares and anxieties of everyday life. (xxxvi)

Berdyaev finds several thoughts in the apostle Paul of vital importance. One is the concept of resurrection of the body to which we have already referred. Another important Pauline idea concerns the nature of eternal life itself. One does not wait for death in order to live eternally. We could paraphrase a Pauline phrase by saying that "to be spiritually minded is already eternal life." Life in eternity *is*; it is characterized by "is-ness," by one's participation in being, apart from the world of meonic freedom and evil. Also, Berdyaev, as Paul, ties up his idea of paradise or eternal life with the Kingdom of Christ. He tries to give hope even to those who are in hell. "To conquer evil the Good must crucify itself. The Good appears in a new aspect: it does not condemn 'the wicked' to eternal torments but suffers upon the cross." (xxxvii) This cannot be solved by man alone for "it can only be solved through the God-man and grace." (xxxviii) This is the meaning of Christ descending into hell.

Berdyaev has a high place for mystical experience and it becomes evident in discussions concerning life after death. As far back as a pre-World War I work--"The Meaning of the Creative Act"--he expressed himself with vigour on the high place that the mystical experience had in the life of a Christian. In these passages, we see that he established some patterns of thought to which he held over many years. In a much later work, "The Destiny of Man" some of the same concepts are evident. Continuing his observations on mysticism, he sees both Catholic and Orthodox groups as trying to establish "official" mysticisms. He asserts that "mysticism is something deeper than confessional disputes and contrasts." (xxxix) Mysticism, for him, is not to be feared but is the way to a "revival and re-spiritualising of religion." (xl) "Throughout all human history, mysticism has revealed the world of inner man in contrast to the world of the outward man. In various forms these mystical revelations of the inner man have always taught of man's microcosmic quality." (xli) So in one of his major works, "Freedom and the Spirit," Berdyaev indicates that

>...in history the actual relations between mysticism and religion have been delicate and somewhat confused. Religion has been afraid of mysticism and often regarded it as a source of heresy, for mysticism was in some way a hindrance to its organising functions and threatened to upset its recognised standards. But religion, nevertheless, needed mysticism and sanctioned its own particular form of it, as the very crown of its own life. (xlii)

We see the clear connection between mysticism and eternal life when he presses the point that

>In mystical experience man always escapes from the isolated sphere of the soul and comes into contact with the spiritual source of being and divine reality...Mysticism is the depth and height of the spiritual life; it is one of its qualities...It must be continually repeated that

> mysticism is not a state of romantic subjectivism,
> for it is above the antithesis between the subjective
> and the objective. Nor is it a dreamy condition
> of the soul. It is essentially realistic and sober
> in the discerning and discovery of realities.
> The only true mystic is one who sees realities
> and knows how to distinguish them from phantasies.
> (xliii)

It is through this experience that the Christian is able to achieve a continuing experience of eternal life. It is not that one becomes one with God, or unites with God but that one senses a oneness with the spirit of God, an immanence, a dwelling of that spirit. Mysticism, as Berdyaev interprets it, treads a narrow ridge and cannot be put into a tight framework.

> The very foundation of mysticism is an inner kinship
> or union between the human spirit and the divine,
> between creation and the Creator. It implies the
> overcoming of transcendence, and that sense of
> God and man being external to one another. Thus
> mysticism is always concerned with the immanence
> rather than the transcendence of God, an immanence,
> moreover, which is actually experienced.... (xliv)

With Berdyaev, his mysticism keeps God and man separate while permitting man to experience eternal life. And it points beyond our existence here in the natural world. Mysticism, he maintains, "shows us that the transcendental opposition between God and man, man's consciousness of his infinite smallness, and the isolation of the natural world, are not final truths, nor the definitive expressions of the mystery of life and being." (xlv) Mysticism then leads us to final reality, and through it we are able to achieve the life divine, the life eternal.

> Mysticism frees us from the natural and historical
> world which lies outside us, and brings the whole

> evolution of material nature and history within the sphere of the spirit. To live through anything mystically is to live through it spiritually and from within. In the practise of mysticism the whole objectified external world is blotted out in the night of sensibility, and it is only within the spiritual and divine world that anything is revealed. Final reality is only revealed in mysticism, in which man escapes from the secondary world of reflections and symbols. All that in religion, theology, and worship was symbolic and only prefigured in the flesh, becomes real in mysticism, and is revealed as the inner depths of life in its basic and original form. It is only in contemplation and mystical union that the divine life is achieved. (xlvi)

After several points, the same message is emphasized, that this is the way to a new nature. "Man is transfigured and deified only by an inward reception of the Holy Spirit." (xlvii) Mysticism is the new birth in the Spirit. That is what all the mystics teach us." (xlviii) There are dangers and he continues to warn his readers. "Phantasy in this sphere in life may easily be mistaken for reality...Mysticism indeed can be illusory." (xlix) His cautions are too lengthy for our use here and do not give us the direction that we need, but they are thoughtful cautions and should be heeded. What we are seeing rather clearly is that Berdyaev moves in the direction of belief in the possibility of a new birth for a Christian not through logic or proofs though his thinking is quite logical and reasonable. He sees this through the movement of the Spirit upon man, and of our movement towards the One of the spirit.

Berdyaev is a thinker who sees paradise as beyond the time world and in the realm of eternity. And the mystical experience for him is a way to reach that eternal life. The narrow ridge comes back to haunt us for "we must not live the 'world,' in the Gospel sense of the word, but rather escape from its domination, though at the same time loving divine creation, the cosmos, and man himself." (1) He also warns that though mysticism may well bring this new life in the spirit that "mysticism cannot become the organising principle of the life of mankind or of whole nations. It is for this reason that it is often in conflict with the sort of religion upon which this task or organisation devolves." (li)

There is throughout Berdyaev's writings an aura of hope even when he discusses hell for the victory is not just for those who have found eternal life. We see him reaching out for those who have not found the way. His is a life of participation in love that is in some ways more implicit than explicit in his writings, but it is there nonetheless. As one reads in Berdyaev, one comes away with hope not despair, and a strange sense of assurance that this man has remarkable insights about its nature.

Once again, his approach is tied up with the Gospel of John, with Pauline mysticism and with the spirit of love. We find these strains repeated here as elsewhere.

> The Christianity of St. John is one of life and is opposed to that hardening of heart which is commended by patristic writers and the ascetical mystics. We are bound to love all created things, the whole of God's creation, and every human being, and it is precisely personality that we should love in God and through God....For there is a mysticism of love, the apostle of which was St. John, and equally too St. Paul. (lii)

One does see in all this a life of tension as well as peace. For to live eternally one must not be so attached to things, and this world and time that one cannot participate in the world of eternity. But in love, Berdyaev sees a clue to a resolution. Our love for created things is not so much a love for things as it is for God's creation.

And our love for one another is a kind of participation in another's life that death does not destroy for it has and does participate in being itself, in the depths of eternity.

> No solution indeed is possible except in the love of Christ and in the fulness of love...The supreme goal of mysticism is not only union with God, but also, because of this very union, a turning outwards of the self towards every creature. It is the realisation of love and of creative energy, for love is creation. In this way the command of Christ to love God and man is fulfilled. (liii)

Eternal life then is not for oneself but, in the spirit of love, is a dwelling with God and the eternal spirits of those we also love. In his references to some of his own experiences we do see remarkable intimations. We do find confusions at times, but only rarely statements that are contradictory. **Some apparent differences of positions** are no doubt due to a growing, changing mind. In spite of this, there is a remarkable consistency in Berdyaev's writings all the way from his early writings during Czarist days to his later writings out of lively philosophical and religious discussions in Paris.

A very remarkable existential passage that pertains well to our subject at hand is Berdyaev's description of his reactions when his much loved wife died after a great deal of suffering. Once again, even in this dark moment, the note of hope and confidence is present. We need to include here two important paragraphs from this account.

> Lydia fell seriously ill with paralysis of the throat muscles; she could hardly speak or swallow food. Her physical strength was declining with each day, but she bore this agonising illness in a wonderful way. At the end of September 1945 she died. Her death was a source of great illumination as well as of burning pain for me. I have never known anyone inspired by such faith on the

threshold of death. Her mind and consciousness remained clear until the very end, everything she wrote (she always wrote, since she could not speak) before her death reflected her intense spiritual vision....Her words seemed like a direct testimony of remarkable spiritual insight and experience. I do not cease to recall what I have lost in her and what I learnt from her during those last months. I cannot be reconciled to death and the tragic finality of human existence; and my whole being resists the notion, naturalised by Heidegger, of death as the ultimate reality. There can be no life unless it restores all those we love to itself.

But this concerns one aspect of death only, death as a thief, a taker away of what is most valued; but there is another, a more luminous aspect. For death may be the triumph of self-sacrifice and love. Man finds it hard to face the mystery of death, but he also comes to know in death a unique value which is love issuing in eternal life. Life must be lost before it can be fully won. Love and death are inseparable, but love is stronger than death. That is why in death communion with those we love continues and is even intensified, for it has passed through the supreme sacrifice of love which is death. When Lydia told me on the eve of her death that she would always be with me, I knew that this was true. Death is an event in time and a token of the power of time over man; but it is also an event bringing him face to face with and issuing in eternity, in which love and kinship are victorious over estrangement and disunion. (liv)

In one way this sounds strangely like some passages in Gabriel Marcel that we shall be examining. It is also part of Berdyaev's ethical relevance and philosophy of interrelationships. He sees that his life in paradise cannot be possible except as there are others also participating. And this concern reaches even other forms of life and some objects that we usually think of as inanimate. "My salvation is bound up with that not only of other men but also of animals, plants, minerals, of every blade of grass--all must be transfigured and brought into the Kingdom of God." (1v)

CHAPTER IV
Gabriel Marcel

Gabriel Marcel is a fascinating French writer who has some very special ideas to add to our understanding of life after death. Known in Europe for his plays, many of his writings, as with other existentialists, are in journals. However he did lecture and, at points, wrote at length on the subject. One solid lecture on "Death and Hope" is at the close of his second series of Gifford Lectures given at Aberdeen, Scotland in 1950. He was very bilingual and lectured also in the U.S. And in his lectures, he often illustrated them with scenes from his plays. If we are to understand him we must first see his two types of reflection--primary and secondary. Though he sees that there are things in life we can analyze and prove, that they may well not be the center of a vibrant life. Relationships cannot be so proved yet may be the most important aspect of our life.

It is quite possible that we lose something in the translation of the words. The words that Marcel uses: "reflexion primaire et reflexion seconde" do carry the approximate meaning of the English words used in the translation of his works. We will continue to use the words commonly used in translations of his works but a French professor friend suggested to me two other words that could possibly be used that might be less confusing. He said that if he were doing the translating, he would use the phrase "initial reflection" for primary reflection and "subsequent reflection" for the term secondary reflection. His idea does seem to be clearer. It will help us to realize that, for Marcel, these words are not used in a meaning of value judgment which would give first importance to the word "primary." They are used in an enumerative manner indicating that the primary reflection may well be the initial relationship, not the most important.

Primary reflection, for Marcel, refers to problems that may be solved, to the world of analysis and objectivity. Some thinkers do try to deal with the existence of God, with our own natures, and with

questions about immortality in an objective, problematic manner.
Marcel sees this approach weighed in the balance and found wanting.
There is no doubt but that these objectives, analytical writings do
have considerable value. It is just that in the light of Marcel's
position, these writings have a serious lack. When we deal with these
matters Marcel would insist that there must be an existential ring,
not just strict objectivity. And so it must lead to the world of
mystery as he calls it. When we discuss death or the possibilities
of any form of life beyond that event, we must consider the existential
possibility of your death or mine. It is our own death that is an
impending event. So, if we follow his reasoning, we will be driven
to the necessity for participation. There is, obviously, much merit
in analysis and in some matters, a good measure of objectivity. But
Marcel reminds us in strong terms of the extent to which we are involved
in the milieu we are discussing.

Gabriel Marcel's position and ideas about immortality may pose
some serious problems for us. His views are not rigidly presented
for he has no rigid system. But out of his exisential framework,
we can trace some concepts that are central and out of which he traces
his ideas of life after death.

In an essay on "Participation," Marcel has some important biographical entries. One concerns the death of his mother and speaks for
itself.

> Beyond all question the sudden death of my mother
> gave me a lasting shock and aroused in me an anxious
> questioning. I could not tolerate the equivocal
> position into which my family seemed to fall.
> I clearly recall a certain walk with my aunt when
> I must have been about seven or eight, during which
> my aunt, having told me that no one could know
> if the dead were completely annihilated or lived
> on in some way, I exclaimed: 'When I'm older I'm
> going to try to find out!' And I think it would

be a mistake to take those childish words lightly: in some way they determined the course I was to take. (i)

(This entry was from his first William James lecture at Harvard University in 1961.)

A much earlier writing, from his "Metaphysical Journal" (1914), gives some notes of this thinking at that time on immortality. Here we see the important personal reference of thoughts on this subject and also his direction which places the inquiry in the realm of mystery, not of verifiable fact. In an entry for February 1917, Marcel says that "by definition immortality falls outside any possible verification. Verification brought to bear on the beyond brings it down to the place of earth; this immortality is only <u>by</u> and <u>for</u> faith: the spiritual order is such that we are bound to think of it as transcending the accidents of matter; we only participate in the spiritual order on condition we think in this way...belief in immortality like belief in God is involved in the very act of our freedom." (ii) Hence, as he continues he asserts that "the problem of immortality has to be stated in personal terms." All of this reflects a general position that goes quite to the center of Marcel's thinking. He ties it up with a position of the Italian philosopher Pietro Prini and calls it "the methodology of the unverifiable." And Marcel says that this may be found as far back as his unpublished writings of 1912 and 1913, where he says that his concern was "to define a positive and concrete unverifiable and to show that it was the source of love and faith." (iii) The dimension to which he refers is an apprehension of <u>presence</u>, an apprehension that many have avoided as a consideration in thinking.

...it is proper to take as a point of departure certain very simple and immediate experiences, but the philosopher up to our time has always had a tendency to neglect them. For instance, we can have a very strong feeling that someone who is there in the room, very close to us, someone whom we see and hear and whom we can touch, is nevertheless not present. He is infinitely farther from us than such a loved one who is thousands of miles away or who even no longer belongs to our world. What then is this presence which is here lacking? (iv)

This presence, as Marcel views it, renews one from within, and is an experience of revelation. "This presence is in such a case revelatory: it makes me be more fully myself than I would be without it." (v) We shall probably understand this even more clearly when we see the distinction between problem and mystery in Marcel's thinking. Since this experience of presence has essential meaning both with the relationship of one person to another and the relationship of one person to being itself, Marcel sees this also as an important quality of love. Marcel speaks of eternity and the spirit of love much as he does later in one of his plays and then also in the Gifford lectures. "I tried to get beyond this dilemma by having recourse to love and by saying that 'love wishes for the eternity of its object.'" (vi)

Marcel's thinking on this subject does make a significant contribution for he thinks in a fresh way and from premises that are involved with life and loving. It is important for us, if we are to understand his special reference and his distinctive contributions, to summarize briefly some of his essential concepts. It is also important to note in passing that though, for thirty-nine years of his life, Marcel had no Christian commitment, he did come to a major decision about the Christian faith at that time, and his later writings do show an influence. It is not that he read his ideas into Christian documents, but rather that his reading of Christian documents added new dimensions to his thinking. His views may not represent the traditional Christian doctrines, but he is convinced that his views are Christian. Vincent Miceli points out that up to that day of decision on March 5, 1929, "Marcel had been more attracted by Protestantism than by Catholicism.

He felt that Catholics were not free. Whenever he conversed with his Protestant brother-in-law, a pastor in the village of Ardeche, he felt himself closer to him than to his Catholic friends. Thus, he could not explain why he chose Catholicism in answer to Mauriac's appeal." (vii)

Certain central affirmations appear and are important for us to sort out. His strong emphasis on intersubjectivity is important for our thinking about eternal life as he sees it. One of the most basic affirmations of this occurs in a 1937 essay "My Fundamental Purpose" where he says that "Something powerful and hidden assures me that <u>if the others do not exist, neither do I</u>..." (viii) A few pages later in the same essay he continues saying "that the philosopher, as I conceive him, ought to push to its limit the desire for communication" because "philosophically, the road which leads from me to the other passes through my own depths." (ix) In his "Metaphysical Journal" (1938-1943) reproduced in the same volume, Marcel comments on the way some can transform the being they love into a thing and "which in effect turns out to be lost. With this thing, I could not form a veritable 'we'; and if there is an indestructibility, it is only by starting from the 'we' that I can succeed in thinking about it." (x)

This basic concept of intersubjectivity is at the root of his views on immortality and is also the root of Marcel's hope. "One may very well, for example," he continues in another section, "speak of the light of knowledge. I will even say that one is bound to do so. Failing this, epistemology itself becomes dry and distorted....One could say that intersubjectivity is the face of being together in light." (xi) In fact, the more one searches for meaning in Marcel, the more one is confronted with the certainty that all the major issues are for him "a question of relational life." (xii)

Marcel puts himself at quite a different point from Descartes with his base--"I think, therefore I am." Marcel is saying that we begin not with an "I" but a "we." At first it is the primitive "we" state of baby and mother. The "we" state expands and one has a family, later a sense of community. The relationship is the real world for Marcel, a world where we participate and therefore not a world we can take apart, analyze and prove. And for him, life after death also must be a life of relationships, not a world of proofs.

Secondary reflection deals with the unknowable or with matters that cannot be settled by analysis, those matters of concern beyond verifiability. It involves "mystery" but Marcel does not use this word as we commonly use it. He means by this word to embrace the world of reflection about those relationships in which we are involved and from which we cannot separate ourselves including our participation in Being itself. Mystery then is not, for Marcel, a problem beyond knowledge but the realm of participation that is beyond subject and object. Immortality, for him, falls into this realm of mystery and participation. So we find it difficult to stand apart and to think objectively about death and immortality for we, the thinkers, the doubters, the believers, are also those who will "put on immortality" or face the angst of the threat of non-being. Hence, as we speculate on life after death and develop beliefs about it, Marcel would say that we find ourselves in the world of secondary reflection (or subsequent reflection) and the world of participation in being, not the world of objectivity and analysis. It was as early as 1910-1914 that Marcel wrote that "metaphysics is above all a philosophy of participation....It is the participation of thought in being that we are here concerned with." (xiii)

In "Creative Fidelity" Marcel shows a dimension of this point of view as he discusses our approach to considering our own nature. He indicates that, insofar as we only analyze that just far, we may miss the most significant dimension of our being.

> 'Who am I? You alone really know me and judge me; to doubt You is not to free myself but to annihilate myself. But to view Your reality as problematic would be to doubt You, and, what is more to deny You...' (xiv)

The way to approach this, then, according to Marcel is through the "methodology of the univerifiable." We might add, parenthetically, that William Ernest Hocking in his expanded lectures (Ingersoll and Thomas lectures) on immortality comments that

> Gabriel Marcel has performed a clarifying service in adopting the term 'mystery' for a type of issue in which the inquiring self becomes part of the datum for its own inquiry, distinguishing it from the term 'problem' which indicates a challenge to the ingenuities appropriate to science and technology: such ingenuity has no part in the issues of death and continued life. (xv)

Marcel maintains with vigour that an objective view of life after death must fail.

> ...love vanquishes death; it negates death. Will someone object that this 'true survival' remains empirical and in fact forms a part of the order of truth, of the verifiable order, that it can be false? But it must be absolutely denied that any verification is possible. Death withdraws the individual from the order of verification, of possible experience--and it is in this sense that affirmation of a real afterlife cannot be false....The affirmation of an afterlife is therefore linked to love, and cannot be separated from it; as soon as survival is posited as an objective fact, it becomes a pure figment of the imagination which has nothing to do with metaphysics. (xvi)

However, in "Creative Fidelity," a work which Marcel regarded as "the best introduction to his thought," we see another brief reference that is helpful.

> If what I have said is true, a philosophy of transcendence must never divorce itself <u>even in principle</u>

> from a type of reflection which is directed on the hierarchy of the various modes of adoration, culminating not in a theory, to be sure, but rather in an understanding of saintliness; a saintliness apprehended not as a way of being, but as something given in the purest form of its <u>intention</u>. The fact that it is here and here alone that the problematic is overcome, and that in such a life the imminent presence of death is abolished in the fullness of being itself. (xvii)

The strength of the factor of participation cannot be underlined too much for it has implications for Marcel's philosophy of interrelationships and also for his views on life after death. Marcel was convinced that through participation, one recognizes another as essence, as being. And this conviction is central to an understanding of the direction that he took about immortality.

> It seems that the more a being has been recognised, greeted by me in his essence as being, the less he is in fact confused with the detailed view that circumstances have permitted me to see of him; the more in fact I have been able to recognize his value, that is today, something that can be illustrated only within experience, but which goes infinitely beyond these illustrations. I have said 'value.' Another way to describe it would be 'essence.' However, we would do well to guard ourselves against the temptation to objectify. Let us remember that it is here a question of a relational life. (xviii)

David Roberts adds some clarification to this idea by indicating that being is indestructible and participation in it—a participation of relation is a way to participate in that which always is. "Participation in the reality for which one sacrifices himself means that the significance and worth or personality-and-community are indestructible; for Being is indestructible." (xix) Later on the same page, Roberts continues: "Hence, so long as we confine the discussion to whether immortality is a fact or a delusion, we have not touched the heart of the matter. Factual evidence has to do with people insofar as they are objects. Whether the factual evidence is taken to indicate that these objects are destroyed or survive, nothing has been said about the person as a Thou." So, the Thou is concerned with the We and participation in that which is Being and indestructible and immortal. For Marcel this concept is also tied up with his meaning of "presence" and "intersubjectivity." This intersubjective presence, for him, is not an objective relationship but one of participation, a relationship that we cannot view from without. In "Presence and Immortality" it appears this way:

> Intersubjectivity is essentially an openness...It would be important to go into it and to bring out its implications. It seems that they emerge only in a philosophy of light. I take this word in a meaning much akin to that which is given to it in the Gospel according to St. John...One could say that intersubjectivity is the fact of being together in the light. (xx)

Marcel's belief in immortality follows in this very strain, the line of presence and participation and intersubjectivity. Eternity does involve the survival of one's identity, but not as an objective ego; it involves a relation, a bond, a form of participation in the eternal. It is a relationship that is beyond "thingness."

One of the areas of central significance for understanding Marcel is to affirm that in thinking of life after death that we cannot think of our death in isolation. We live in constant relationships. From birth, through life, and death, we live in a constant web of relations. And when we die, we change in our relationship to those about us. We may continue some of these relationships, this is a possibility.

In one way, none remain the same. But Marcel would say that, insofar as we participate in being, in that which itself is indestructible, so far we may be immortal. Some relationships then, in their essence, continue. Nevertheless, some memory relationships do change. It is also clear that by Marcel's thought structure, insofar as we have a life after death, this too involves ongoing relationships, relationships to those who also have died, and those who yet live, and to the Creator God who gave us life and will give us hope. For a Christian, these relationships may involve a relation with the Risen Christ and to the members of the Christian community.

Marcel is not trying to wreak havoc with identity situations. In fact, this is a good part of his concern. But somehow he wants more than a <u>survival of a part</u> and seeks to think of immortality of all that we are. Of course, this is never fully possible since in death our bodily functions do cease. Marcel struggles to show his concern for <u>all</u> we are, yet he does see the difficulties. He comments in his "Philosophy of Existence": The <u>I am</u> is, to my mind a global statement which it is impossible to break down into its component parts."

Perhaps another part of this consideration is that in Marcel we find little, if any, mention of heaven, and certainly hell has no apparent place in his thought. Life after death then is certainly not a time of either punishment or reward for this French thinker. In one of his "Philosophical Fragments," notes that were written during 1912 and 1913, he writes that "The crass realism which place God before the soul as an exterior judge before a defendant cannot be seriously envisioned." (xxi) It is a continuing world of relation in being and so perhaps the only punishment (or reward) might be in the lack (or presence) one might sense because we do not (or do) know the depths of subjectivity. In his discussion, this deep relationship is bound up with hope and communication and freedom also. In a later chapter in the same work Marcel continues his thought in this wise: "It is true in a general way to say that the quality of a being can be recognized and proved by the fidelity of which he is capable.... Moreover, fidelity cannot be humanly exacted, anymore than love or life. I cannot force another to reply to me, and I cannot even force him in reason to hear me, and it will always be possible for me to think that if he does not reply it is because he has not heard me.... It is because fidelity is creative that, like liberty itself, it infinitely transcends the limits of what can be prescribed." (xxii) Some of these distinctions will also become more clear as we deal later with Marcel and his idea of love.

Not all relations, including human relationships, are on a profound level. Some human relations, as Martin Buber as well as Marcel has pointed out, can be "I-it" relations, relationships when the other is regarded as an object or a thing. Marcel adds that "we must fully realize that this being whom I love is not only a Thou; in the first place he is an object which comes within my view..." (xxiii) This form of relation is not an indestructible one, but is rather ephemeral. "It is not, I think, from the noumenal point of view that the indestructibility of the loved being can be affirmed: The indestructibility is much more that of a bond than that of an object." (xxiv) The persistence of a relation is a fundamental part of Marcel's thought. Human love, according to him, is "charged with infinite possibilities." (xxv) This is a central characteristic of love itself, that it has infinite possibilities. So when the apostle Paul says that "love will never cease," he is not repeating a simple platitude but is affirming a very essential thought. Marcel is emphatic that immortality is not and cannot be a delusion or a mirage for central, affirmative love is enduring. Love endures in that it brings us not only into relationships with each other in a profound way but also brings us into participatory relationships with being itself.

Once a living, loving relationship is established, it is eternal. "...Whatever changes may intervene in what I see before me, you and I will persist as one: the event that has occurred...cannot nullify the promise of eternity which is enclosed in our love, in our mutual pledge." (xxvi) The elements of mystery within a relationship of depth defy analysis and can point to "some substratum of reality which eludes our sight." (xxvii) Once again, in this same lecture, Marcel uses a play reference to make his point "as concrete as possible" as he says. "First let me quote again what one of my characters says, 'to love a being is to say, Thou, thou shalt not die.'...From the point of view of the empiricist or positivist it could only be considered absurd, for is it not in effect in formal contradiction with the data of experience?" (xxviii) He does admit that insofar as the one I love participates in the nature of things there must be some destruction. But, continues Marcel, "the whole question...turns upon knowing whether this destruction can overtake that by which being is truly a being. Now it is this mysterious quality which is aimed at in my love." (xxix) In his "Phenomenological Notes" (in "Creative Fidelity"), Marcel adds that "we transcend one another in the very heart of our love." (xxx)

William Ernest Hocking has some passages that sound much like these we find in Marcel, passages where he links the concept of love to that of immortality.

> And thus to love is to treat the loved being as worthy of permanence....I propose that here, in willing to confer immortality on another mortal, the self is in that moment reaching a deeper self-consciousness, an intimation of its own destiny....And since the unrealized but germinal self has the dimension of infinitude, <u>the mission of love in time is never done</u>. (xxxi)

The one important difference here is the phrase "in time" for neither Marcel nor Berdyaev would agree at that point.

In Marcel's thinking, immortality is not some vague ongoing of one's influence. It is a kind of personal immortality for one does participate in that which is eternal. It is actually a kind of "inter-subjectivity unity which is formed by beings who love one another and who live in and by one another." (xxxii) Marcel's idea of life after death must include others, relationships and also some personal identity that is always involved in relations (and relations with other identifiable individuals). It does appear that some Christians would want to agree with this, for many conceive of life after death in terms of recognition and enduring relationships. Marcel sees these as so important for the good life that it is inconceivable for us to think of God as a creator on the one hand and as a destroyer of relations on the other. It is possible then to move from this to a conception of relating to one another eternally in some genuine relationship. "This is what we more or less explicitly mean when we assert our faith in personal immortality. What we must do, then, is to discover whether I can assert that this holy God is capable either of ignoring our love, or treating it as something accidental or devoid of significance, or even of decreeing its annihilation." (xxxiii) We are created out of God's love, must live in the spirit of love and so how could one imagine this ever ceasing to be? "But is it conceivable that a God who offers Himself to our love, should range Himself <u>against</u> this same love, in order to deny it, to bring it to nothingness?" (xxxiv) For Marcel, "the affirmation of an afterlife is therefore linked to love." (xxxv)

David Roberts has some words that try to clarify the position of Gabriel Marcel in his chapter on him in a work published after Roberts' death:

> Marcel replies that the Christian hope does not rest upon the outcome of a factual inquiry. The factual evidence for survival is not only meager (probably non-existent), it is religiously well nigh irrelevant; for the most it could show, even if it were strong, it would be the survival of the ego, whereas what Christian hope is directed toward is not merely survival, which might still be egocentric, but life in God. Hence so long

as we confine the discussion to whether immortality is a fact or a delusion, we have not touched the heart of the matter. Factual evidence has to do with the people insofar as they are objects. Whether the factual evidence is taken to indicate that these objects are destroyed or survive, nothing has been said about the person as a Thou. (xxxvi)

In "Presence and Immortality" written in 1951, Marcel attempts once more to clarify this distinction. He asserts strongly that we may participate in the presence of one and that this does not have to be linked with objectivity. He cites, only briefly, some work in telepathy not to <u>prove</u> survival, but only to indicate that those who work in that field show "us that here exist modes of co-presence which are irreducible to the type of juxtaposition involved in our everyday dealings with other men. Those who have most seriously reflected on telepathy for example—I am thinking of Carrington, and also of Price—have recognized that such phenomena imply a kind of specific unity among beings." (xxxvii) We may assume here that he refers to Hereward Carrington, one-time director of the American Psychical Institute and author of such works as "Mysterious Psychic Phenomena" (xxxviii) and H.H. Price, whose paper on "The Problem of Life After Death" was read at a meeting of the Society for the Study of Theology in Nottingham, April 1967 (and has received considerable attention).

Marcel also sees some of these "modes of co-presence" when he turns to the world of music (for he too was a composer and playwright as well as a philosopher). "It suffices to recall the way in which amelodic idea arises for example. It occurs to us, takes hold of us; where does it come from? Does it come from myself or from somewhere else?" (xxxix) The presence of which Marcel is here speaking is he says "supra-hypothetical," and he says it is "connected with oblative love." He reinforces this by saying that

> I am assured that you are present to me and this assurance is linked with the fact that you do not

> stop helping me, that you help me perhaps more directly than you could on earth. We are together in the light. More exactly, in moments when I am detached from myself, when I cease to eclipse myself, I gain access to a light which is your light. Surely I do not mean the light of which you are the source, but that in which you yourself blossom, that which you help to reflect or radiate upon me. (xl)

Marcel ties this sense of presence, the spirit of oblative love, and hope for immortality together. There are some fuzzy areas that might have been helped with stronger definitions. But it is part of his viewpoint that definitions too precise may take one to the world of analysis and proof and primary reflection. He relies at times on allusions, sometimes in references to plays and to music and he hopes that we the readers will understand. David Roberts interprets Marcel as avoiding another dualism and clarifies his asssertion in this manner:

> ...he declares that to construe his statement as an attempt to divide the person into a destructible phenomenon and an indestructible noumenon, is to misunderstand the case entirely. For this is to remain within the patterns of objective thinking, separating man into 'parts.' But the indestructibility he has in mind is that of a meaningful <u>bond</u> rather than an object. The quality and promise of eternity can be enclosed in the love that exists between two people.... Participation in eternity is claimed for such a human bond, not as a closed system between husband and wife, parent and child, or friends, but as reflecting, under conditions of finitude, a divine love which charges existence with infinite possibilities. (xli)

The contrast is there--the world of structure and precision and analysis and the world of mystery and participation. For Marcel hope lies only in the one sphere and it is this world of mystery that breaks through and enables us to conquer death.

> This world of ours is so structured, that I can find around me every reason for despairing, for seeing in death the annihilation and the miserable keyword of the incomprehensible existence into which I have been senselessly thrown. But to a deep reflection, this world appears simultaneously as being so constituted that I can become conscious in it of the power I retain to withstand these appearances, to deny the death of this ultimate reality. (xlii)

When we begin to explore this world of mystery further we find Marcel often using the word love in describing what he sees there. And a precise definition may elude us but we can see some parameters. There is a rather negative definition in one of his plays when he says that "because I love you, because I affirm you as being, there is something in you which can bridge the abyss that I vaguely call 'Death.'" (xliii) There is an area of ambiguity it is true, but there are some statements that do help to sharpen up what he really means. His Gifford lectures help us:

> ...from the moment when my affirmation becomes love, it resigns in favour of that which is affirmed, of the thing which is asserted in its substantial value. This is precisely what love is; it cannot be divorced from this resignation. In other words, love is the active refusal to treat itself as subjective, and it is in this refusal that it cannot be separated from faith; in fact it is faith. (xliv)

He continues illustrating what he means from a longer play plot summary and then adds that "as soon as one loves or is loved by another being, an awesome solidarity comes into being between the two." (xlv) It is, over and over gain, this solidarity that Marcel believes partakes of being and is eternal.

In some early notes, Marcel does wrestle with the nature of this viewpoint, arguing that this is not just an immortality in thought but a participation in transcendence. It is an important statement:

> For my immortality cannot be thought directly by me. I can think of myself as immortal only insofar as I am myself the creation of an act of love. It might be objected that this comes down to saying: I can think of myself as immortal only in the loving thought of others. This conclusion, however, is utterly false. Such a solution is contradictory and useless, because the afterlife which is an object of faith involves an act of transcendence which negates what, to reflection, appears as its own subjective conditions of elaboration... Thus it seems that my faith in my own immortality has a bearing upon the identity of the individuality which I create in myself and upon this creation of love whose survival others will affirm by faith. (xlvi)

The way in which Marcel prefers to describe some of his convictions in this matter is through expressions which are not really precise, yet they convey meaning. In some late essay published in France in 1968 under the title "Pour une sagesse tragique" and in 1973 in American as "Tragic Wisdom and Beyond," Marcel quotes from one of his play characters. (This is from a play never performed in France at the time he wrote this essay.)

> There is one thing I discovered after the death of my parents—that which summons us to survive [survivre] is actually what sustains us [sousvivre]. And those whom we have never stopped loving with

> the best of ourselves become like an immense skyscape, invisible yet somehow felt, under which we move forward, always more divided from ourselves, toward the instant where everything will be enveloped in love. (xlvii)

In these ways, we are beginning to identify some of the salient characteristics of love as Marcel sees it. It is not the love that Sartre speaks about, maintaining that it destroys the freedom of the person being loved. Marcel's use of the word "oblative" signals to us that it is an offering spirit, not turned in on itself. In the deepest meaning of the New Testament agape, it centers on a full caring for the other. Marcel would say that possessive love speaks of death, oblative love of life. For him, love is the source of hope and the root of his belief in life after death. "Now, we must assert as forcibly as possible that human love itself is nothing, it lies to itself, if it is not charged with infinite possibilities." (xlviii)

That such a state does give hope, Marcel is confident. But he is also not one to outline clearly the characteristics of that life beyond death, as Berdyaev was, for example. He speaks of it only in terms of a "beyond," "with infinite possibilities," and as a state of oneness with being. This "beyond" is a state partially apprehended here in our moments of reaching beyond the world of things and sense, in moments of great music, and of great loving and caring for another. But beyond death, it may be fully apprehended.

Though Marcel does not underline often the distinction between his view and that of Sartre, it is there rather clearly. Sartre says in "No Exit" that "hell is other people" because, as he sees it, other people are possessive and seek to destroy my freedom. For Marcel, oblative love is not possessive but is bound up with freedom and fulfillment and may lead to our deepest hope. Since his Gifford lectures were given in 1949 and 1950, Marcel ties up his discussion of hope and the lack of it with the plight of some prisoners of war. Hope, he says, is not just liberation from captivity but seeing ourselves as captives and seeing the dimensions of our captivity. "To hope is to carry within me the private assurance that however black things may seem, my present intolerable situation cannot be final; there must be some way out." (xlix) Hope then is not just hope for oneself. Hope is bound up with love and is hope for the fruition of relationships at their best. "Hope was not simply a hope for one's own self; it meant spreading one's hope, keeping its flame a radiance of hope burning around me...each man's personal reality is itself intersubjective." (l)

Hope, for Marcel, must not be about specifics and particularly hope for onself only. He therefore interprets the phrase "to hope that" to indicate more specific hopes, and hopes for oneself. Hope must be hope for "us," for the continuance of a relationship which is, according to him, the way to participate in being itself. This is an emphasis found in Homo Viator and he comments on himself in the later Presence and Immortality.

> Hope on the other hand is not egocentric: to hope, I have written in Homo Viator, is always to hope for us. Let us say that hope is never the state of wishful thinking which can express itself by an 'I would very much wish that.' Hope implies a prophetic assurance which is really its armor and which prevents the being from breaking down, internally first of all; but it also prevents him from giving up... (li)

It is important to cite here that the world of hope, for the existentialist Marcel, is "ultimately installed in a region which transcends that of 'facts.'" (lii) Kenneth Gallagher's fine book on Marcel's philosophy continues at this point to expand on this concept and relate it to the important idea in Marcel of presence and the problems of verifiability. Some experts from one especially forceful page in Gallagher's work should add important dimensions to our thinking at this point.

It is a <u>presence</u> which evokes hope, not accumulation of probabilities. Borne up by a communion whose very atmosphere is eternal, unreservedly disponible to the Absolute Presence which enfolds this communion, the soul moves ceaselessly beyond the reach of critical thought; and this movement reveals the 'intelligible core of hope....

Then why cannot the process be a grand illusion? If hope offers no arguments and does not admit of being verified, then what guarantees its truth?.... This way of putting questions remains imprisoned in a mode of thought which must conceive subject and object as external to each other. It is always then possible to wonder whether the object is as 'really real' as the autonomous subject which questions it. Hope, however, knows nothing of such an object: it arises in the recesses of a presence which it is strictly impossible for it to regard as external to itself. Hope is an 'unverifiable,' if one likes, but no more so than any mode of awareness that bears on presence.... The foolproof world of the problematic, for instance, can exercise a fatal attraction for a certain type of temperament which finds satisfaction in its endless stretches of sheer certitude and tends to view hope as a scandal of the intellect and an embarkation across an unknown sea.... Hope is metaproblematic: as an act it is no longer possible to dissociate it from that on which it bears. (liii)

Marcel carries this same emphasis one step further by suggesting that as we view death, it is not just a specific death that matters but the death of one we love. One wonders how far he can carry this emphasis. "What matters," he continues, "is neither my death, nor yours; it is the death of the one we love...the only essential problem is posed by the conflict between love and death...where love persists, where it triumphs over whatever tends to degrade it, death cannot be definitively vanquished." (liv) There are other thinkers who strike similar chords. William Ernest Hocking ties up his ideas of love and interrelationships with the view of the immortal self in one of his Ingersoll lectures at Harvard:

> The durability of the self...must depend on the truth of its interpretation of love--itself a riddle deeper than that of the Sphinx...for love...is also in its promise a power to become immortal.... (lv)

When we attempt to understand the dimensions of love as Marcel intends to use the term, one of the most helpful treatments of all is in a section of Gallagher's work on Marcel's philosophy. Marcel himself relates intersubjectively as central to his ontology and also as the act of love itself. Gallagher adds that love

> ...does not bear on a closed essence, but rather opens on to an infinity--a presence which no tabulation can exhaust love reaches the being of the beloved, and not merely an idea of him...love is beyond the subject-object dichotomy... The intimacy of love is a primary mode of being, irreducible to any other... (lvi)

It is this relationship to being, the ontological aspects of love, that has a bearing on beliefs about life after death. Gallagher expresses Marcel's ideas about this by saying that "the more we love him, the more we comprehend him as authentic being, the more we can be assured of his perpetuity.... Really to love a creature, Marcel would agree, is to live him in God. Only in the absolute does the promise of eternity with which all love is redolent attain to unconditionality." (lvii)

Marcel's philosophy of intersubjectivity is not a humanistic approach if we see it fully. His direction is a theistic one, and we see this in his Gifford lectures as he struggled with the rejection of theism and belief in life after death at the time he was writing them (1950). This statement (following) reveals several things including his rejection of ideas of survival as egocentric, and his insistence on a theistically grounded idea of relationships.

> We seem to be saying that the modern world has chosen death, but should not one rather say that under the impulse of positive science on the one hand, and perhaps also on the other, of a philosophy which on the whole one may describe as critical, the keenest minds have been forced to discard as imaginary the dreams of the beyond, of the so-called hereafter, in which our ancestors found consolation? There will be some who will take up a different point of view and add that they would consider it excessively unwise to tie the fate of religion to a belief in a fact as problematical and improbable as survival--not only imprudent but even spiritually illegitimate, since preoccupation with survival is still ego-centric, whereas a religion worthy of the name finds its centre in God and in God alone. (lviii)

For Marcel, then, there is hope, but it is not a hope for survival in what he fears might be an egocentric sense, but a hope that rests in God primarily, not with man, though it involves a thorough subjectivity. In the next lecture, he continues this in another way, relating his position to that of Pascal and also Kierkegaard and speaking of finding ourselves "when we are in the presence of God." (lix) The quality of life is most important, as it appears also in Berdyaev's discussion and in passages from the apostle Paul. For there are persons who are biologically "alive" but are spiritually dead. "On the other hand we have all met people who remained alive in the spiritual sense until the verge of death, and when their physical strength seemed utterly exhausted." So the relationships continue--with new emphasis on the quality of those relationships so that they, in the spirit of oblative love, may lead one to participation in being itself.

In summary, then, we do see him saying positive things about life after death and relating it to the ongoing intersubjective relationships we develop here. He sees these relationships as participating in the world of transcendence and the realm of being. These relationships of love cannot be ephemeral for him. They are born of our freedom, our very freedom to live. And he cannot conceive of a God who creates us out of his love and then annihilates the creation of love. So out of his theism and his profound philosophy of intersubjectivity, Gabriel Marcel leaves us with a certain view of the future and immortality, one rooted in the spirit of love and eternal relationships. Though we may be critical of him at points, it is difficult not to see in his closing words of the Gifford lectures a kind of symphony itself, or harmony that may be forever.

> Let me make use again of one of the musical comparisons for which you know I have a taste, and say that from the moment when we open ourselves to these infiltrations of the invisible, we cease to be the unskilled and yet pretentious soloists we perhaps were at the start, and gradually become members, wide-eyed and brotherly, of an orchestra in which those whom we so inaptly call the dead are quite certainly much closer to Him of whom we should not perhaps say that He conducts the symphony, but that He *is* the symphony in its profound and intelligible unity; a unity in which we can hope to be included only by degrees, through individual trials, the sum total of which, though it cannot be foreseen by each of us, is inseparable from his own vocation. (lx)

CHAPTER V
Paul Tillich

Two recent books on eternal life both find little hope in Paul Tillich. But as one reads these volumes, one looks in vain for any solid understanding of this great twentieth-century theologian. Paul Badham has only a fleeting reference to some few pages in Tillich's first volume of sermons. Dr. Badham's tutor, John Hick, has more to say but we must add that he does not explore the depths in Tillich. Hick ends up with sentences that say that Tillich leaves one with "intellectual confusion. On the one hand he rejects the notion of the continued life of an individual beyond the grave." (i) In this chapter we shall maintain precisely the opposite--that though his mind grew and writings changed he does not leave us in confusion. And we see him with strong hope in Christian faith of eternal life.

Who is this man? Many do not ask for he is still widely read and new books on him still appear nearly twenty years after his death (1965). Books about him fill an entire file drawer in the Cornell University Library card files. A stout opponent of Nazism, his position as a distinguished professor at Frankfurt was taken from him. He came to America at the invitation of both Columbia University and Union Theological Seminary. He worked hard to make his English understood and in the decade preceding his death he lectured to thousands on many university campuses. Retiring from Union, he became a University Professor at Harvard when he retired from the post, he then went to the University of Chicago and at age 79 was about to take a new post at the New School in New York City when he died of a sudden heart attack. His writings are vast and one can only wish that his closing volumes of his "Systematic" had come out earlier. He was always open to criticism and other views and therefore was a remarkable teacher who first wanted to see where you were and help you from there, never imposing a system upon you.

As a student of Paul Tillich while he taught at Union Theological Seminary in New York City, I could see two major sides to him. He

did have many sides as any full person does and we see some of these in the splendid appraisals of Rollo May and of Marian and the late William Pauck. The two major aspects of this thought I saw might be summarized in this way:
1. The German philosophical theologian who was a precise, clear teacher and writer.
2. The mystically inclined, devout Christian who could witness as well as describe.

In one way one could describe the Tillich of the chapel as "beyond argument." Though one may criticize such a statement, it may still stand as a description of Tillich the preacher in a chapel. It was not that his sermons were erratic or ill-prepared. They are instead remarkable essays, the product of a great mind. But in chapel, Tillich was not argumentative, nor did he seek to present a series of arguments (such as Reinhold Niebuhr was prone to do, for example). In Tillich, the mystical strain kept reasserting itself. If we are to understand his sections on life after death, God as being itself, and essentialization (among other concepts) we must see the central place that mystical experience and participation has in Tillich's thinking. It was not only evident in his "Systematic" but in repeated passages in the transcribed notes of lectures (that I heard in person) now entitled "The History of Christian Thought," and also in his Ingersoll lecture on immortality given at Harvard in 1962.

My growing conviction has for some time been that one needs not only his more analytic passages in the "Systematic" but also the more mystically oriented approach in some places in the same volume, and also in his sermons and some other writings, if we are to be fair to his position. This was greatly reinforced when I secured a copy of Tillich's Ingersoll lecture (a work not circulated very much since it never appeared in book form). In more than one place in this lecture, Dr. Tillich sees the distinction between the mystical and the prophetic approach to understanding the world of life after death.

In the Ingersoll lecture, he is striving to recover the richest meaning of the word "mystical" and to avoid distortions that have grown up around it.

> One may call this the mystical experience, if the word mystical is kept free from such distorting connotations as foggy, irrational, emotional, etc. which have made the word almost useless; but we need an abbreviation for the way in which countless billions of people in the history of mankind, especially in the East, have experienced the ultimate meaning of live. So let us keep the word mystical. (ii)

In the Union Seminary series of lectures (History of Christian Thought), Tillich raises the issue with his students whether or not mysticism may be baptized by Christianity and he is certain that it is possible insofar as it becomes a Christ-mysticism. It is quite clear as Carl Braaten points out that "without the mystical element in religion Tillich observed that it becomes reduced to intellectualism or moralism." (iii) This places Tillich in opposition to both Barth and Brunner who did reject the place of mysticism in the Christian faith. In one lecture, Tillich said that

> The meaning of mysticism has been misinterpreted by Protestant theology which began with Ritschl and is still alive in Barthian theology.... Every medieval scholastic was a mystic; that is, he experienced what he was talking about as personal experience. This is what mysticism originally meant in the realm of scholasticism. There was no opposition between mysticism and scholasticism. Mysticism was the experience of the scholastic message. The basis of the dogma was unity with the divine in devotion, prayer, contemplation, and aescetic practises. If you know this, it may be hoped that you will not fall into the trap of removing mysticism from Christianity....

> Mysticism--the Protestant Orthodox theologians call it <u>unio mystica</u>--is the immediate union with God in his presence. (iv)

(Throughout this chapter especially, we want to keep in mind that Tillich was a thinker whose thought underwent creative changes right up to the time of his death. So we need to keep this changing creativity in mind. These lectures on "Christian Thought" and his Ingersoll lecture came at about the same period around 1962.)

Paul Tillich has no single work as such that deals with either his views on mysticism or his concepts about eternal life (except for the Ingersoll lecture on immortality). We must find them in many of his writings. With a few perplexing exceptions, most passages are quite clear and so we are convinced that we are not distorting his views by pulling them from diverse works. In one very important section in a lecture found in "The History of Christian Thought," Tillich sets forth his place in the world of mystical thinking perhaps as definitely as at any point.

> Although I am not a mystical theologian, I would say that I am more on the side of the theology of experience and inwardness, for I believe that the Spirit is in us. In the concept of the Spirit the highest synthesis is given between the Word of God which comes from the outside and the experience which occurs inside...the theology of inner experience...is frequently but wrongly called 'the inner Word.' That is not a good term. 'Inner light' is better. In modern terminology we speak of 'existential experience.' (v)

Tillich also continues this discussion by indicating that reason and mystical experience do not have to conflict but that they have a relationship. For Tillich,

> ...the principles of reason develop out of an originally ecstatic experience which produces

> insight. This insight can become rationalized.
> As the principles of reason emerge within us, the
> original underlying ecstasy can disappear or recede,
> with the result that the Spirit becomes Reason
> in the largest sense of the concept.... The opposite
> of mysticism is not rationalism, but rationalism
> is the daughter of mysticism. (vi)

In discussing the Middle Ages, Tillich did see the place that ascetic practice played. But he does not see this actually as an integral part of the center of the true mysticism. When he tries to define or clarify the word, he sees the frequent distortions.

> A person, for instance, is said to be a bit mystical
> when he is somewhat foggy in his mind. That is
> not a serious usage of the term. Mysticism means
> inwardness, participation in the Ultimate Reality
> through inner experience.... This mystical element
> is the inward participation in and experience of
> the presence of the divine. (vii)

It is this sense of presence of the Divine that was most evident with Tillich in his chapel messages. And we find this participation in the Spirit as a central thought in his "Systematic" as well. There is a parallel with Gabriel Marcel as Tillich explores the possibility of going beyond the subject and object world and into the direction of unity with Being itself. We may summarize some of one paragraph in his section on "The Divine Spirit":

> ...in spite of all antimystical tendencies in Protes-
> tantism, there is no faith...without the Spirit's
> grasping the personal centre of him who is in the
> state of faith, and this is a mystical experience,
> an experience of the presence of the infinite in
> the finite... [This does include] the mystical
> as a category, that is, the experience of the
> Spiritual Presence. Every experience of the divine

> is mystical because it transcends the cleavage
> between subject and object, and wherever this
> happens, the mystical as category is given...both
> faith and mystical experience are states of being
> grasped by the Spiritual Presence. (viii)

Tillich wrestles with this problem of mysticism and what he terms "self-salvation" and deals at one passage (in Vol. II) with "mystical attempts at self-salvation." He sees it necessary to make some differentiations about the word "mystical" and to draw conclusions after these distinctions are made.

> 'Mystical' is, first of all, a category which characterises the divine as being present in experience. In this sense, the mystical is the heart of every religion as religion. A religion which cannot say 'God himself is present' becomes a system of moral or doctrinal rules which are not religious, even if they are derived from originally revelatory sources. Mysticism, or the 'felt presence of God,' is a category essential to the nature of religion and has nothing to do with self-salvation. (ix)

For Tillich we find (in both the "Systematic" and his Union lectures) that "mysticism can be 'baptized' in which the mystical experience depends on the appearance of the new reality and does not attempt to produce it." (x) This is, in the light of the Pauline tradition, a Christ mysticism, a mysticism of being "in Christ."

All of this emphasis in Tillich has special reference to our study as we realize more and more the central place for him of the importance of participation. Regeneration, Tillich says, "is the new state of things, the new eon, which the Christ brought; the individual 'enters it,' and in so doing he himself participates in it and is reborn through participation." (xi) Tillich sees Barthian theology as an approach from the outside of man, and that his existential approach begins with man himself and not with "outside" concepts. Insofar as he has a conceptual base for his thinking here it is thinking about the divine Spirit and here Paul Tillich follows Paul the Apostle for "Paul was the great theologian of the divine Spirit." (xii)

It may help at this point to draw some generalizations. First, Dr. Tillich is concerned with the individual including the individual's participation in life after death. Secondly, there is little interest in the whole matter of punishment and reward. He does see on the one hand the persistence of dual threats of "death away from eternity" and the contrasting "promise of eternal life" but that is about as close as he comes. Thirdly, Dr. Tillich is a thinker of hope who has a strong confidence in life after death. We find this evident, not in a single treatise, but in many places, in his "Systematic," in several sermons and particularly so in his Ingersoll lecture on immortality delivered at Harvard University.

One other valuable insight into Tillich's thought comes from Rollo May's book on him. He tells of his "dying day" as Tillich himself called it. It concerns a dream that Dr. Tillich had on this final day and that he recounted to his wife Hannah. A strange man addressed him and in a kind voice told him that someone was about to die. "Is it Rene?" Tillich asked. And there was a nod. But someone else was also dying. "Is it Hannah?" and once again there was a nod. May comments that "The dream seems to me to come out of his great loneliness on that final day. Such a dream also reflects the archetypal mode of meeting the loneliness by taking family members with one in death." (xiii)

It is also true that, for Tillich, the central reference finally is not man, but God and he tries to interpret this in some fresh terms. At the center are such phrases as "the Ground of our being" and "our Ultimate Concern." In fact, Tillich is theistic in his own way yet he discounts the traditional proofs for the existence of God. It is, he says, "as atheistic to affirm the existence of God as it is to deny it. God is being-itself, not a being.... As the power of being, God transcends every being and also the totality of being--the world." (xiv) Earlier in the same volume he puts it even more bluntly: "God does not exist. He is being-itself beyond essence and existence. Therefore to argue that God exists is to deny him." (xv) Since he often refers to God as eternal, his theistic views are important for us in our understanding of his views on eternal life. Discussing "Eternal Life and Eternal Death" Tillich centers thought in this wise: "everything as created is rooted in the eternal ground of being," and "everything comes from eternity and must return to it." (xvi) Though this last quotation does not imply life after death, other quotations will subsequently make these relationships clear. Here we are only concerned to show the relation between Tillich's concept of God with his concept of eternity and also with his views on life after death as eternal. A most important quotation at this point summarizes the relation of God to being:

> Since God is the ground of being, he is the ground of the structure of being. He is not subject to this structure; the structure is grounded in him. He *is* this structure, and it is impossible to speak about him except in terms of this structure. God must be approached cognitively through the structural elements of being-itself. These elements make him a living God, a God who can be man's concrete concern. They enable us to use symbols which we are certain point to the ground of reality. (xvii)

In a later volume Tillich centers his thought on God as eternal, and ties this thinking up with a Pauline view. "How is the eternal God, who is also the living God, related to Eternal Life, which is the inner aim of all creatures? The only possible answer is that Eternal Life is life in the eternal, life in God." This corresponds to the assertion that everything temporal comes from the eternal and returns to the eternal, and it agrees with the Pauline vision that in ultimate fulfillment God shall be everything in (or for) everything.

It is possible to call this symbol "eschatological pan-en-theism." (xviii)

> God is eternal; this is the decisive characteristic of those qualities which make him God. His is subjected neither to the temporal process nor with it to the structure of finitude. God, as eternal, has neither the timelessness of absolute identity nor the endlessness of mere process. He is 'living,' which means that he has in himself the unity of identity and alteration which characterizes life and which is fulfilled in Eternal Life. (xix)

Preaching a sermon on Hebrews 2:14-18, Tillich puts this in a strong light that the path by which we are to participate in the eternal is through the One who has power over death. So, as an Advent sermon, he finds that the coming of the Christ means just this, or should mean this to us. The sermon concludes with these words:

> Do not deceive yourself about the seriousness of death--not death in general, not the death of somebody else, but your own death--by nice arguments for the immortality of the soul. The Christian message is more realistic than those arguments. It knows that we, <u>really we</u>, have to die; it is not just a part of us that has to die. And within Christianity there is only one 'argument' against death: the forgiveness of sins, and the victory over Him who has the power of death. It speaks of the coming of the Eternal to us, becoming temporal in order to restore our eternity. The whole man is mortal and immortal at the same time; the whole man is judged and saved at the same time, because the Eternal took part in flesh and blood and fear of death. That is the message of Christmas. (xx)

We catch one more indication as to Tillich's direction of thought when he seeks to differentiate between immortality and resurrection.

(we may note in passing that Dr. Cullman does this with even more clarity in a paper that has received much attention.) (xxi) Dr. Tillich says that at times the symbol of immortality is used to express what he calls a "popular superstition," namely "in the non-Christian pseudo-Platonic form of a continuation of the temporal life of an individual after death without a body." (xxii) Insofar as the word is used in that way, Tillich says it must be rejected by Christians. There is another use, he says, that in a very few New Testament passages where the word may carry another meaning. He refers, for example, to I Timothy 6:16 where the word for "immortality" that is used there is interpreted by some as "no death." "He is King of Kings and Lord of Lords; he alone possesses immortality, dwelling in unapproachable light." Tillich interprets this passage as saying "if the term is used in the way in which I Timothy 6:16 applies it to God, it expresses negatively what the term eternity expresses positively; it does not mean a continuation of temporal life after death, but it means a quality which transcends temporality." (xxiii) This would then have some relevance to Paul's phrase "to be carnally minded is death, but to be spiritually minded is life and peace." (xxiv) This is a strong interpretation of eternal life as a quality of life here and now that could continue beyond the event of death.

When Paul Tillich preached a sermon on "The Eternal Now" he made it clear (much as Berdyaev would say) that "endless future is without a final aim; it repeats itself and could well be described as an image of hell." (xxv) He is not comfortable either with the phrase "hereafter" nor "life after death," saying that the Bible does not use this language. And he chides the writers of the liturgies who speak of "world without end." "But the world, by its very nature, is that which comes to an end. If we want to speak in truth without foolish, wishful thinking, we should speak about eternal that is neither timelessness or endless time.... There is no time _after_ time, but there is eternity above time." (xxvi)

The sermon is directed to the anxiety of the awareness of one's end. The Eternal is that which overcomes this, gives us hope and enables us to find the dimension of "presence." "It is the eternal that stops the flux of time for us." (xxvii) Our age--or at least the age to which Tillich was speaking--"lacks the courage to accept 'presence' because it has lost the dimension of the eternal." (xxviii) The closing of his sermon includes his words of hope that he sees through the power of the eternal. "There is one power that surpasses the all-consuming power of time--the eternal: He Who was and is and is to come, the beginning and the end. He gives us forgiveness for what has passed. He gives us courage for what is to come. He gives us rest in His Eternal Presence." (xxix)

As one reads Tillich with care, it becomes apparent that he also finds Platonic dualism in opposition to a Christian view of the resurrection. He says that a concept of immortality "introduces a dualism between soul and body, contradicting the Christian concept of Spirit, which includes all dimensions of being..." (xxx) In a later section, he cites the Old Testament as bascially anti-dualistic but notes that it subscribes to the idea that the body belongs to Eternal Life. Tillich feels that the apostle Paul sees some difficulty in this position and tries to modify it, calling the resurrection body "a spiritual body." So he says "Spirit--this central concept of Paul's theology--is God present to man's spirit, invading it, transforming it and elevating it beyond itself. A Spiritual body then is a body which expresses the Spiritually transformed total personality of man." (xxxi) Earlier in the same volume, Tillich begins his most serious discussion of his concept of Spirit and is quite strong at the very outset that "soul" is a lost concept, one that lost much of its meaning when it became regarded as an immortal substance that was rejected by modern epistemology. He finds this rejection still strong in modern psychology. Paul Tillich does not see the necessity to resume the word "soul" but seeks the meanings of the word "spirit":

>Spirit does not stand in contrast to body Life
>as spirit transcends the duality of body and mind.
>It also transcends the triplicity of body, soul,

and mind, in which soul is actual life-power and mind and body as its functions.... Life as spirit can be found only in man, for only in him is the structure of being completely realised. (xxxii)

Paul Tillich sees that the word for soul has still some meaning particularly in poetry where he sees it "designating the seat of the passions and emotions" but he continues his rejection of the concept especially in an evolutionary sense. Though some would disagree, Tillich is convinced that the nature of spirit which puts man above the animals does not mean that "at a precise moment of the evolutionary process God in a special act added an 'immortal soul' to an otherwise complete human body, with this soul bearing the life of the spirit." (xxxiii) On the other hand, he does see a two-fold nature of man; this is the aspect of our nature that is important for understanding Paul Tillich. Life, he asserts, "is ambiguous because it unites essential and existential elements. The essential or potential in man and his world is the source from which the norms for life in the dimension of spirit are derived." (xxxiv) God is beyond this contrast (xxxv) but as we deal with the nature of man, it is an important distinction as we deal with Tillich's thought.

One of the ambiguities in the above quotation leaves us wondering about the words "soul" and "spirit." Actually Paul Tillich is quite clear about this, but is clearest in this third volume of the "Systematic." He did admit one time to Nels Ferre that by the time he wrote that third volume (actually quite late in his life), he was moving away from discussing "being" in favor of using the word "Spirit." (xxxvi) It is also true that in the third volume, Tillich becomes clearer in his definitions and puts the words "spirit" and "Spirit" and "soul" in clearer focus with regard to this thought.

Dr. Tillich begins his discussion of these words by pointing out the derivations in Greek, Latin, German and Hebrew (in order): <u>pneuma</u>, <u>spiritus</u>, <u>Geist</u>, and <u>ru'ach</u>. Then there are other confusions, particularly in English, with the customary usage of "Spirit" for the divine, and "spirit" for man and a dimension of his life. He raises the serious questions whether or not "the word 'spirit' does designate the place in our psychological language." Here "the word 'soul' has suffered a fate similar to that of the term 'spirit.' It has been lost in human endeavor which calls itself the 'doctrine of the soul,' namely psychology. Modern psychology is psychology with psyche." (xxxvii)

When it comes to a more complete definition of the word for his use, then Tillich defines the word spirit in this wise:

> If spirit is defined as the unity of power and meaning, it can become a partial substitute for the lost concept of soul, although it transcends it in range, in structure, and especially, in dynamics. In any case, while the word 'soul' is alive in biblical, liturgical, and poetic language, it has lost its usefulness for a strict theological understanding of man, his spirit, and its relation to the divine Spirit. (xxxviii)

In a sermon on "Spiritual Presence" Tillich says that "Divine Spirit means: God present to our spirit" and then adds that "Spirit is not a mysterious substance.... It is God Himself...God as present in communities and personalities, grasping them, inspiring them, and transforming them." (xxxix)

The importance of this for our study is clearly that, for Tillich, the vital aspect is to cite the importance of spirit in the life of man and to insist that our spirit may participate in the life of the Divine Spirit and the Divine Spirit may break through into ours. Tillich does underline the necessity for seeing man as an integral whole and yet he does find ways later to indicate that our essentialization may go on even after the demise of the body. At this point in his discussion, he emphasizes the many sides to our lives and yet our essential unity. And he sees that a concept of spirit helps to maintain these views better than the traditional view of body and soul.

> These considerations reject implicitly the doctrine that at a precise moment of the evolutionary process God in a special act added an 'immortal soul' to an otherwise complete human body, with this soul bearing the life of the spirit. This idea--in addition to being based on the metaphor 'level' and a corresponding supranaturalistic doctrine of man--disrupts the multidimensional unity of life, especially the unity of the psychological and the spirit, thus making the dynamics of the human personality completely incomprehensible. (xl)

For him, this "principle of multidimensional unity denies dualism as well as psychologistic (or biologistic) monism." (xli) What he is seeing as a possibility is life with both essential and existential elements and a life process that moves in three directions: self-integration, self-creation and self-transcendence. (xlii) The spirit is a vital aspect of our nature and the essentialization of our spirit continues as it participates in eternal life. Many passages in Tillich may be viewed as an illumination of Pauline passages. For example, Tillich finds the Pauline concept of "spiritual body" a most helpful symbol and quite in line with what he calls the "anti-dualistic bias of the Old Testament." The apostle Paul, so Tillich points out, realizes the difficulty of the symbol that "the body belongs to Eternal Life" and sees "the danger that

> it may be understood in the sense of a participation of 'flesh and blood' in the Kingdom of God...And against this 'materialistic' danger he calls the resurrection body 'Spiritual' ...A Spiritual body then is a body which expresses the Spiritually transformed total personality of man. One can speak about the symbol 'Spiritual body' up to this point; concepts cannot go beyond this, but poetic and artistic imagination can. And even the limited

> statement which is made here points more to the
> positive implication of the double negation than
> it does to something directly positive. If we
> forget this highly symbolic character of the symbol
> of resurrection, a host of absurdities appears
> and conceals the true and immensely significant
> meaning of resurrection." (xliii)

In many ways, the thought of the apostle Paul is a source and confirmation of Tillich's thought. He not only finds rich meaning in the "Spiritual body" concept but also in such phrases as "the new birth" or regeneration.

> In biblical and theological literature, the state
> of being grasped by the Spiritual Presence is called
> 'new birth' or 'regeneration.' The term 'new birth'
> (like the Pauline term 'New Creation') is a biblical
> precedent to the more abstract concept of New Being.
> Both point to the same reality, the event in which
> the divine Spirit takes hold of a personal life
> through the creation of faith. (xliv)

Tillich also adds that the liturgical phrase "resurrection of the flesh" used in some creedal forms should be replaced by the more biblical phrase "resurrection of the body" and this should be interpreted in a Pauline manner as the symbol "spiritual body."

There is one sense in which the more philosophical terminology of Paul Tillich about essence and existence may parallel the concepts in the apostle Paul about the "level of the spirit" and man's "lower nature." In both cases, these men are talking of a kind of fulfillment of one's essential nature. Paul expressed it this way: "Those who live on the level of our lower nature have their outlook formed by it, and that spells death; but those who live on the level of the spirit have the spiritual outlook, and that is life and peace." (xlv) Dr. Tillich adds that "the New Being is not another being, but the transformation of the old reality, arising out of its death." (xlvi)

And one may rightly puzzle if there is not some kinship with Jesus' story of the prodigal when he had come to himself." (xlvii) Translated as "coming to one's senses" (N.E.B.) it is speaking of the same transformation.

In his discussion on Eternal Life, Tillich refers, even if briefly, to "essentialization." In the light of Tillich's whole existentialist outlook, this phrase carries considerable meaning and weight. In his first volume of the "Systematic," a volume dedicated "To My Former Students Here and Abroad," he is rather insistent that Christianity "<u>must</u> deal with the problem of being, for, although essence and existence are philosophical terms, the experience and the vision behind them precede philosophy. They appeared in mythology and poetry long before philosophy dealt with them rationally. Consequently, theology does not surrender its independence when it uses philosophical terms which are analogous to terms which religion has used for ages in prerational, imaginative language." (xlviii) For Tillich, then, this is not regarded as an abstract philosophical problem but rather as a recurring problem of one's existence.

It is equally clear that this has an integral relation to his views on "eternal life." Life beyond the event of death has an important reference to this also. "All dimensions of life were included in the consideration of the ultimate <u>telos</u> of becoming." (xlix) The important passage to which we have reference includes the following:

> Resurrection says mainly that the Kingdom of God includes all dimensions of being. The whole personality participates in Eternal Life. It we use the term 'essentialization,' we can say that man's psychological, spiritual, and social being is implied in his bodily being—and this in unity with the essences of everything else that has being. (1)

When he says that this "includes all dimensions of being" and that Eternal Life involves "essentialization," we may possibly assert that Eternal Life is life in the essence. It is more than an existence.

Some of the same distinction appears in Berdyaev, but much more explicitly expressed. This phrasing of Tillich's hints at some creative ideas, full of possibilities for thought. "It does not yet appear what we shall be..."

Tillich ties up his views on essence both with the life to come and with our fallen state. As he states, "essence as the nature of a thing, or as the quality in which a thing participates, or as a universal, has one character. Essence as that form which being has 'fallen,' the true and undistorted nature of things has another character." (li) This essence as the central nature of a person is the center which enters into eternal life. This much is clear. This is for Tillich the meaning of the Pauline concept of the resurrection of the body. And he is convinced that one may think of this in a non-dualistic way.

> Aristotle has shown this possibility in his ontology of form and matter. If the soul is the form of the life process, its immortality includes all elements which constitute this process, though it includes them as essences. The meaning of the 'immortality of the soul' then would involve the power of essentialization. (lii)

Here Tillich is moving in two directions of thought. This particular quotation is intended largely to indicate that in Aristotle (and he adds some notes about Plato also) one finds a non-dualistic approach to thinking about "the soul as the form of the life process." The other side is that he is commenting on the use of the phrase "life hereafter" as found in I Timothy 6:16. He says that this "does not mean a continuation of temporal life after death, but it means a quality which transcends temporality." Later on, he attempts one other interpretation to indicate how the transformation takes place. This time, Tillich uses the figures of finite and infinite and interprets the Pauline passage that He can "clothe our mortality with immortality" saying that this means that "our finitude does not cease to be finitude, but it is 'taken into' the infinite, the eternal."

One more step becomes clear in his discussion for this emphasis "also includes a strong affirmation of the eternal significance of the individual persons' uniqueness." (liii) And later in this chapter when we summarize Tillich's Ingersoll lecture, this emphasis once again becomes prominent. "Individual persons always were in the center of eschatological imagination and thought, not only because we ourselves as human beings are persons, but also because the destiny of the person is determined by himself in a way in which it is not under the dimension of life other than that of spirit." (liv) Paul Tillich was very personally oriented as I knew him, oriented to specific individuals, and so when he writes of eschatological hope, it has this personal reference. It is not a statement about a hope for being in general but for an individual person. As one proceeds with his discussion of this aspect of eternal life, he affirms some important things about the eternal destiny of the individual with respect to eternal life. Eternal life, he states, "is life and not undifferentiated unity" and therefore "the self-conscious self cannot be excluded from Eternal Life." (lv) Tillich is not unmindful that the question is often raised "with respect to the eternal destiny of the individual" about "the presence of the self-conscious self in Eternal Life." (lvi) He comments that even if we think of participation as a prime description, "there is no participation if there are no individual centers to participate." (lvii)

He adds two other statements, negative ones but important ones, about this matter: one, that "eternity transcends temporality and with the experienced character of self-consciousness" and secondly, "the self-conscious self in Eternal Life is not what it is in temporal life." (lviii) These seem almost self-evident statements that might add little to one's concept of life after death, but they may reinforce the conviction that Paul Tillich did think of life after death as he thought of life in very personal terms. What I see him doing is interpreting Christian symbols and thought forms about life after death, but not negating them. In his later works particularly he is quite strong in his emphasis on eternal life.

A section in Hammond's work on Tillich adds some important clarifications and also affirms our contention here that Tillich does see eternal life for the individual. The positive aspects, Hammond says, are found in Tillich's concept of life.

> Tillich understands the final or eschatological movement as 'essentialization,' or that movement which brings finite existence to fulfillment. This consummation involves the actualization of essence or potentiality enriched by the struggles and conflicts of existence in freedom.... In Tillich's view everything positive is gathered up into the divine life; nothing of value is lost. (lix)

Hammond extends his argument to state forcefully that, for Tillich, the individual continues in eternal life.

> What then is the destiny of self-conscious selves? The realization of individual centers of consciousness is a good which must be taken up into the transcendent unity of the divine life. In Tillich's view individuality is not eliminated in eternal. It is preserved in polar relationship with universal participation (or unification). In other words, the unity in the eternal is in the form of life, where individuality is the prerequisite for interpersonal union. (lx)

It is also clear, says Hammond, that for Tillich "the conscious self is not preserved in the same form as in earthly existence." (lxi) If, for some, this means the end of personhood, then one would have to admit that Tillich would not envision the continuation of a conscious self as one knows the conscious self in this life. He sees the process of essentialization and individuation continuing but changed. To say that "the conscious self is not preserved in the same form as earthly existence" is not to say that some form of consciousness does not continue. There must be some affirmation of a change in state or there would be no meaning in death. As Tillich says in his "Systematic Theology":

> As the participation of bodily being in Eternal Life is not the endless continuation of a constellation of old or new physical particles, so the participation of the centered self is not the endless continuation of a particular stream of consciousness in memory and anticipation. (lxii)

Clearly, this does pose problems for some persons who insist more on a continuation of a memory process than he envisions, but he is making a point that there is a significant change in the life eternal. He continues:

> ...The self-conscious self in Eternal Life is not what it is in temporal life.... As the New Being is not another being, but the transformation of the old being, so resurrection is not the creation of another reality over against the old reality but is the transformation of the old reality, arising out of its death. (lxiii)

In summary, then, we may say that, for Tillich, that which continues is that aspect of us that participates in being, that which is eternal, not the time-conscious self but a transformed self not fully participating in eternal life. Resurrection, then, for Tillich, refers to the transformation that takes place bringing one fully into the life eternal. Tillich does say: "Resurrection is not the creation of another reality over against the old reality but is the transformation of the old reality, arising out of its death." (lxiv)

This puts Tillich at quite an opposite pole from views of Sheol with individuals almost "lost" in the world beyond death, for, as he sees it we become, as individuals. "What we shall be has not yet been disclosed." (lxv) The New Being is the fulfillment of the essence that we are; it is the fulfillment of eschatological hope. One might wish that Tillich had used more positive statements instead of his negative ones in this discussion. But this in itself may be significant. For this may well be his way of indicating that we may state negatively what we believe about life after death with more assurance than we can state these beliefs positively. "As the participation of bodily being in Eternal Life is not the endless continuation of a constellation of old or new physical particles, so the participation of the centered self is not the endless continuation of a particular stream of consciousness in memory and anticipation." (lxvi) With respect to his two negative principles, Tillich is surprisingly dogmatic when he says that "everything said which exceeds these two negative statements is not theological conceptualization but poetic imagination." (lxvii)

This negative approach is one we find when Tillich discusses, even briefly, his views on heaven and hell. In Berdyeav, one finds long and almost detailed elaborations about the nature of the life beyond. Tillich does not give such elaboratiaons, but in a negative way is rather clear that he does not subscribe to literal ideas about heaven and hell.

> If something is, if it has being, it is included in the creative divine love. The doctrine of the unity of everything in divine love and in the Kingdom of God deprives the symbol of hell of its character as 'eternal damnation.' This doctrine does not take away the seriousness of the condemning side of divine judgment, the despair in which the exposure of the negative is experienced. But it does take away the absurdities of a literal understanding of hell and heaven and also refuses to permit the confusion of eternal destiny with an everlasting state of pain or pleasure. (lxviii)

Part of his discussion seems to lack clarity but has to be understood (if we may understand it at all) in the light of other statements about essence and actualization. In trying to deal with the future life of those who have distorted lives in one way or another, or the problem of a future life of a child who has never had the chance for any actualization, he gives a partially ambiguous answer and then adds some negative caution about predictions of condemnation.

> The question and answer are possible only if one understands essentialization or elevation of the positive into Eternal Life as a matter of universal participation; in the essence of the least actualized individual, the essences of other individuals and, indirectly, of all beings are present. Whoever condemns anyone to eternal death condemns himself, because his essence and that of the other cannot be absolutely separated. (lxix)

Tillich also makes it clear that participation in eternity does involve our relationship with others. Though he emphasizes on the one hand the importance of the self-conscious self in eternal life, and the persistence of the element of individualization, he also shows that those in the community of believers has a relationship with each other. For the believer "must be told that his essence participates in the essences of all those who have reached a high degree of fulfillment and that through this participation his being is eternally affirmed. This idea of the essentialization of the individual in unity with all beings makes the concept of vicarious fulfillment understandable. It also gives a new content to the concept of Spiritual Community." (lxx)

Rather than a life of blessedness or punishment, or a state of endless pain or pleasure, Tillich sees life after death as a resolution of conflict. Each of us has "polar conflicts" of individualization and participation. "In Eternal Life the two poles are in perfect balance. They are united in that which includes the universe of powers of being without annihilating them into a dead identity." (lxxi) Hence Eternal Life is the end of the other polar elements including those of freedom and destiny. Also, if we accept Tillich's definition of religion that it "is the consequence of the estrangement of man from the ground of his being and of his attempts to return to it" (lxxii) then it might follow that in Eternal Life there would be no "religion" as such. "This return has taken place in Eternal Life, and God is everything in and to everything. The gap between the secular and the religious is overcome. In Eternal Life there is no religion." (lxxiii)

The question of the finality of life after death comes back again and again in different writers as we look at them. Each writer has his or her own way of approaching the problem. Most Protestant thinkers do avoid a discussion of purgatory or what it might stand for. In fact, "Protestantism abolished the doctrine of purgatory because of the severe abuses to which clerical greed and popular superstition subjected it." (lxxiv) It was in 1960 when Paul Tillich came to Cornell University to lecture. I arranged with him to have a modest discussion group of local clergy meet with him. During the discussion, he made a quick reference to purgatory saying: "We should develop a Protestant idea of purgatory" but the discussion took other avenues and we never got back to ask what he meant. In a rare passage where he expresses himself on purgatory we find him saying that "Protestantism was not able to answer satisfactorily the problems which originally led to the symbol of purgatory." (lxxv) He sees clearly that the way purgatory is usually conceived, it is carrying the inappropriate concept of time into the world of life beyond death. But one still has not replied adequately to the problem purgatory tries to solve, that is the question as to whether or not one's state is final at the time of death. And Dr. Tillich who did face up to this briefly gives us actually little positive reply also.

There is one other brief reference we can find that gives some hints about Tillich's thinking about this matter. In 1957, he was replying in a magazine article to an essay by Margaret Mead and once more has some reference to the meaning of purgatory for Protestant thinking. He says there that "a Christian motif which in Protestantism has not been taken seriously enough is the question of a possible development of the individual after death.... In the doctrine of purgatory, the Roman Church attempts to answer the question of a developing self after death, and Protestant theologians have talked about a 'state between' temporal existence and eternal life. Perhaps one should be satisfied with the answer that eternal life is <u>life</u>, and therefore not static but dynamic, and that it transcends the three modes of time, reaching back into the past and ahead into the future and experiences (as the gospel of John indicates) in the present: the eternal now." (lxxvi)

The way we approach the end must, according to Tillich, seek the gift of eternal life, given to us by the grace of God. It is not achieved through our struggle and righteousness though we must struggle and also seek to be righteous persons. "The courage to surrender one's own goodness to God is the central element in the courage of faith." (lxxvii) The participation in the New Being is an experience of our acceptance of and by God. The only source for this acceptance is, according to Tillich, "God Himself as Spiritual Presence." (lxxviii) Tillich is sure that Luther would confirm this as the greatest gift of all--"the certainty of being accepted by God." (lxxix) This is the first and major step in the "participation in the New Being, the creation of the Spirit..." (lxxx)

There is a valuable insight in Tillich's sermon on "The Eternal Now" when he says that "if we were totally within time, we would not be able to elevate ourselves in prayer, meditation and thought to the eternal. We would be children of time like all other creatures and could not ask the question of the meaning of time. But as men we are aware of the eternal to which we belong from which we are estranged by the bondage of time." (lxxxi) It is this "eternal now" that gives us a secure hope, not the world of deception that denies that there <u>is</u> an end." (lxxxii) The sermon does not map out specifics for us but it is a sermon of hope. He conveys this by showing how we came from beyond time and can be after time. This is in generalities and leaves us with many questions but it is given with a strong note of assurance. There is hope, he is saying. We will be--for we are sure of the eternal. If we add to this brief sermon, in some sections from the very last part of the final volume of his "Systematic" we have more clarity still. "Eternal Life is life in the eternal, life in God." (lxxxiii) "God, so to speak, drives toward the actualization and essentialization of everyting that has being." (lxxxiv)

A very important lecture that Paul Tillich gave at Harvard (an Ingersoll lecture) has had but little attention since it was never in book form. It is found only in the Harvard Divinity Bulletin but does give some very significant insights to his thought. Entitled "Symbols of Eternal Life," it begins with a clarification of the meaning of the idea of eternity.

> The genuine concept of eternity is not timeless simultaneity; eternity is rather the transtemporal unity of the consecutive moments of temporality. This implies the rejection of the opposite distortion of eternity: its identification with endless temporality." (lxxxv)

This concept has a mystical identity and ties up a creature to the Ground of all. "Despite his belonging to the order of temporality, man belongs to the order of eternity." (lxxxvi)

In section II of the lecture, Tillich sees the central importance of symbols of eternal life, and objects to arguments that attempt to confirm eternal life by empirical knowledge.

> This is the reason why arguments in the context of empirical knowledge can neither corroborate nor refute them. Their language is a religious language and religious languaage is always and by necessity symbolic. It takes empirical material and uses the categories of finitude, especially that of time, to express the dimension of the

> ultimate in being and meaning, but it uses them in such a way that they point beyond themselves. And this 'pointing beyond' makes them symbolic. (lxxxvii)

For Tillich, then, symbolic language has a central role for it becomes "the only possible language for expressing the experience of man's participation in the eternal." (lxxxviii) Here may be seen the importance of participation, an aspect that Marcel too emphasized. Tillich puts participation and individualization in tension with each other. Yet they do not stand as opposites but rather only in polarity. This is a most important point and has relevance also for our discussions on the place of the individual in eternal life.

> There is a basic polarity of all life which can be called individualization and participation. Everything stands under this polarity, and its tension derives from the fact that the more individualized a being is, the more it is able to participate. In man we have complete individualization and universal participation. The symbols of eternal life may be distinguished basically according to the predominance of the elements of individualization or participation. If the participation in the eternal is symbolized by envisioning the finite individual completely drawn back into the Ground of all Being, we can speak of 'symbols of proceeding from and receding into the One.' With the opposite approach we can speak of 'symbols of being created by and reunited with the Ground of Being.' The former belongs to the mystical type, the latter to the prophetic type. (lxxxix)

This does clarify to a point the importance of participation and the role of individualization. Eternal Life, for Tillich, does mean being "drawn back into the Ground of all being."

There are some fine lines to be drawn here and this lecture is of crucial importance in sorting them out. Tillich, in this discussion, covers several attempts to conceive of these two elements in the light of concepts of eternal life. He discusses, though briefly, the Hindu attempts to reach Brahman, and he sees Plato as attempting "to unite individuation and participation" (xc) in a conceptualized mysticism. The doctrine of the immortality of the soul

> ...described the fall of the soul from the realm of the eternal essences to which it belongs into the realm of existence... It also describes the return of the soul to its former state, through a process of individual salvation. The eternal life of the soul which it anticipates in its bodily prison and to which it returns is individual participation in the supra-temporal world. Eternal life is intuition of the essences and ultimately of God. The individual is preserved, but only in its reunion with the eternal. (xci)

Tillich also asserts that especially in contemporary American Protestantism some see the "desirable continuation of life after death indefinitely." (xcii) Insofar as this is true,

> ...the concept of eternal life has been replaced by that of an endless temporal life. The 'life hereafter' is imagined as a bodiless continuation of the experiences and activities of this life. The classical doctrine of immortality has become a popular Christian superstition. (xciii)

If Tillich has any strong assertion about this attitude, he says that "to continue the finite beyond the limits of its finitude is endless punishment and not eternal fulfillment." (xciv)

This is a most helpful lecture to clarify some of his position, particularly on the problems about the concept of the individual and eternal life. For him, this requires drawing some rather careful statements, he says:

> The question, asked most insistently, about the state after death is whether self-consciousness is a quality both of the eternal reunion with the divine life and of the lasting separation from it. To this we must answer that self-consciousness as we experience it in time and space is bound to temporality. Without continually moving and changing perceptions, a state of existence would occur in which the difference between subject and object would disappear. But eternity is not timelessness, and the participation in it is not extinction of the self. As analogy, some ecstatic experiences may be mentioned. The same truth is relevant here as in all our interpretations: you can erect two signposts, but you cannot describe what lies between them. Eternal life is neither continuation nor extinction of the conscious self. (xcv)

He also adds another important clarification which asserts that death itself is not eternal but the absence of eternity or its negation. "And, like eternal life, this is an experience here and now, namely the threatening loss of the meaning of one's life by separation from its eternal Ground." (xcvi) Throughout the lecture it becomes increasingly clear that Tillich puts two symbols in opposition--Nirvana and the Kingdom of God. And there is no question for him that, as a Christian, his symbol must be that of the Kingdom of God. At the end, one can only say this:

> ...the question remains, what about the differences, not only between men, but between all beings and parts of the universe? How to solve the riddle of the unequal capacities for the reception of the light coming from the dimension of the eternal? The answer is given in the third of the symbols

of creation and reunion, the Kingdom of God. The symbol of the Kingdom of God implies universal fulfillment, a new heaven and a new earth, but not in terms of a receding of the universe into its Ground, but in a reunion of all separated and heterogeneous elements of being in the unity and clarity of the divine life. More than this cannot be said. God will be 'all in all,' as Paul expresses it. (xcvii)

Huston Smith has shared with me the account of an interview he had with Paul Tillich in 1959 on "Human Fulfillment" with Tillich discussing some of his views on eternal life. Huston Smith is paraphrasing Tillich's words and Tillich is responding to a query that he says many ask, that is, can the happiness that comes from a deep faith survive bodily death. Smith says that Tillich answered in this way:

>...it would be better if we were so beyond concern for ourselves that the question of our personal survival did not obtrude. But when the question is raised, its answer must be something like this. Eternal life is not future compensation for present privations. It is basically a qualitative term, a term describing life's deepest fulfillment. As such, eternal life is now or it is never. But this does not mean that it is now only. It is now in a way that we can experience, and it endures in an eternity which gathers up and preserves even the temporal aspects of our lives while protecting them against the laws of finite transitoriness. In this sense our final destiny is to have our past, our present, and our future united, without being negated, in the eternal presence. (xcviii)

This discussion of Paul Tillich's views on eternal life may have gone to some lengths but we feel it is needed, partly because he had much to say about it, and partly because there have not been serious treatments of it. We find him a thinker of depth and hope, making solid contributions to our thinking about eternal life.

CHAPTER VI
Some Personal Wrestlings

There are many paths to truth. We have summarized the views of three thinkers who have touched us and given forth insights. Others have been "weighed in the balance and found wanting." This would include John Hick's strange replica theory that John MacQuarrie calls "a remote and even bizarre possibility." (i) It certainly is not biblical in its roots. And though Ernest Becker's work on "The Denial of Death" won a Pulitzer prize, it is a dismal story when he comes to the end. There is little hope in his feeble conclusion: "the most that any of us can seem to do is to fashion something-- an object or ourselves--and drop it in the confession, make an offering of it, so to speak, of the lifeforce." (ii)

Each of the three writers we have presented (in earlier chapters) gives us grounds for hope. None of them have sought to prove the immortality of the soul as Paul Badham does in Cartesian fashion. Some who measure truth by objective and analytical standards, who wish solid, logical proofs, seem at times either to despise or ignore other approaches to truth. Many of the most meaningful relationships in life in which we participate cannot be logically proven, yet we live through them in reasonable fashion. So it is with grounds for belief in life after death. Some bases seem to be reasonable, to "make sense" as we perceive them. Yet there are bases that cannot be proven, which must be assumed and are axiomatical. Certainly there is no way we can approach this subject with the same aura of certainty that is found in mathematical propositions. But even mathematical propositions are based on assumptions and axioms.

Death is a unique event that happens to us. "In the twinkling of an eye," "at the last moment" we are all changed. We are saying here that we cannot return and relate this "experience" as we have been able to relate other experiences. It is our experience of another's death that creates in us an angst about the possibility of our own death. We see its finality in the death of another for we cannot "see" our own death. And this is often the beginning of our pondering.

We are using an approach that is at its heart experiential, but it is not one that seeks empirical proofs. Revelation itself becomes an experiential matter, and so with many insights that are at the heart of mystical religion at its best. Before we construct the more positive grounds for belief in life after death, we should clear the air by discussing other negative aspects of thought so that there is clarity. One often clears ground before building a structure and this may be part of that act of clearing.

1. Heaven, or the life after death, is not a someplace that is somewhere. To say it that way—that it is a "space"—is to use the wrong dimensions of thought. We find ourselves quite in disagreement with Dr. Badham when he says that if we think in terms of a body in heaven that "heaven must be a place" or that "a resurrected body requires to live somewhere." Insofar as it is a spiritual body, then heaven or the life after death must denote a state of being and not a place. Both John Smith, the Platonist, and William Law, the nonjuror, direct us in this way when they say that heaven is within. They are not saying that heaven is only an inner state for they are referring to eternal life and so also to life after death.

2. We find the word "soul" useful but we react against the strenuous effort to prove the existence of the soul as a separate entity and to base one's hope for life after death upon this. We do not seek either to prove or disprove the existence of a soul. One must admit that there is no way to know perfectly what portion of one continues if we believe in life after death. The flesh remains; the flesh decays. This is the part that requires a space. What continues eternally we shall maintain must represent more than a "part." It must be what we are in essence, our true selves. Hence the apostle Paul called this a "spiritual body." This phrase does have stumbling blocks too but we see the concept as struggling to imply more fully a _person_ and not a non-material part. This is a difficult distinction but it must be made.

3. We are not concerned with the world of reward and punishment. It seems strange in a way that attitudes about heaven and hell are so persistent, but they were strong in intertestamental times, are found in some places in the New Testament and certainly Dante aided in the pictorial concept of after-life. Berdyaev may have more to say specifically about this than many others, but his thought is more directed to concepts of eternity and time than any ideas of punishment or reward.

4. We are not seeking proofs for life after death, nor empirical evidence for such life. Rather our search is for gounds for belief in life after death which is quite a different matter. Insofar as we are dealing with bases for such belief, there is an element of experiential intervention into one's life. There is a breakthrough, a revelation, an experience of the presence of the Holy One. For some it is an awareness of the continued blessing of God, of God's goodness and power and love. This is not to seek in the empirical world, but to find ourselves invaded from Beyond in the experiential world.

We do see the need for analytically studying aspects of these viewpoints, but we must affirm that much of what we believe about life after death comes from deep convictions about God's nature and ours. There is much to commend in an approach of holistic perception rather than in seeking meticulous, involved "proofs." It is of note that Hans Küng, who certainly has a remarkably analytical mind, has in his new book "Eternal Life?" closed the pages of affirmation, not argument. The strongest affirmation of eternal life comes, not from the process of logic, but from the depths of perception of one who already knows what it is to live eternally. Küng says it well.

> If I believe in an eternal life, then it is always possible to endow my life and that of others with meaning.... I can rely on the hope that in the eschaton, in the absolutely last report, in God's kingdom, the alienation of Creator and creature,

> man and nature, logos and cosmos, the division into
> here and hereafter, above and below, subject and
> object, will be abolished. God then will not merely
> be in everything, as he is now, but truly all in
> all, but--transforming everything into
> himself--because he gives to all a share in his
> eternal life in unrestricted, endless fullness.
> For, Paul says in the Letter to the Romans, 'all
> that exists comes from him; all is by him and for
> him. To him be glory for ever.' (iii)

So on the one side, we say we are not seeking proofs, and on the other side, God has broken in and we are given hope through the consciousness of the Presence. As Job once expressed it: "I had heard of Thee by the hearing of the ear, but now mine eyes have seen Thee." (iv) This is a different approach than seeking to prove either the existence of the soul, or the possibility of a life in another space beyond the event of death. Karl Rahner in his "Theological Investigations" puts this in rather strong terms: "The devout Christian of the future will be either a 'mystic,' one who has 'experienced' something, or he will not be anything at all." (v)

5. We are not embracing an idea of reincarnation. This has a strange and strong logical appeal, particularly if one begins with the postulate of the immortal soul. For then, "the soul cometh from afar, not in entire forgetfulness," to use Wordsworth's phrase. In the East, Hinduism has given great impetus to this. The New Testament doctrine falls in a different tradition and a considerably different viewpoint than the Eastern one of cycles and Karma and reincarnation. Insofar as resurrection may be a "present" state as well as a future one, then it ends in conflict with reincarnation ideas.

> You are on the spiritual level, if only God's Spirit
> dwells within you; and if a man does not possess
> the Spirit of Christ, he is no Christian. But if
> Christ is dwelling within you, then although the
> body is a dead thing because you sinned, yet the
> spirit of life itself... (vi)

This interpretation of the new life in the Spirit is a far cry from reincarnation.

6. We assert again that must affirm a strong theistic base. Insofar as we have a belief in life after death, it will depend on the measure of our belief in the Ground of our Being. This belief is where we begin, not with the sequence of a logical syllogism. Dr. Paul Tillich put this as strongly as he could when he was lecturing at Union Theological Seminary now some years past. He decried the attempt on the part of some to move by a progressive analysis and proof to:

> ...the existence of a highest being called God. This...I deny; I think it is hopeless and ultimately ruinous for religion. In a religlious statement I could say that where God is not the prius of everything, he can never be reached. If one does not start with him one cannot reach him. (vii)

The same position was echoed by Miguel de Unamano in his "Agony of Christianity." In the essay on his religion he makes it clear:

> I confess sincerely that the supposed rational proofs—ontological, cosmological, ethical, etc.—of God's existence do not demonstrate anything as far as I am concerned: all the reasons given for God's existence seem to me to be...begging of the question.... No one has succeeded in convincing me rationally of God's existence, but neither have they convinced me of His non-existence. The reasoning of atheists strikes me as being even more superficial and futile than that of their opponents. And if I believe in God...it is because...His existence is revealed to me in my heart, in the Gospel, and through Christ and History.... And I will spend my life wrestling with the mystery...for the struggle itself is my sustenance and my consolation. (viii)

The Sarum Psalter is not far from this also:
> God be in my head, and in my understanding;
> God be in mine eyes, and in my looking;
> God be in my mouth, and in my speaking;
> God be in my heart, and in my thinking;
> God be at mine end, and at my departing.

So our lives have their deepest meaning not as the result of strenuous logic, but through an intuitive awareness of the greatness and centrality of That Which Is, the very Ground of our Being. Some root their beliefs about life after death in terms of punitive or reward ideas and so regard God as a severe judge who must be satisfied. But over and over the biblical message is a message of a forgiving God, the very center and root of all we are.

One of the very helpful approaches comes from Gabriel Marcel. Our belief in God and also in life after death, for him, does not come in the world of primary and analytical reflection. This is in the world of secondary reflection for Marcel. In this we confront a mystery, and adopt an existential posture, saying that we cannot be objective about that in which we participate. We may adopt a reasoned and reasonable attitude, but in this area, truth is not arrived at by reason. "Religion within the bounds of reason alone" (to use Kant's phrase) fails one here. It is our participation in Being which is a central concept, central to our understanding of hope for Eternal Life.

The sequence of thought which is important to us here is to move from this general affirmation to affirm further that we are the creatures created out of Love, creatures created to create and to love, creatures in whom abides an inner light that one day may shine brightly, "...the real light which enlightens every man..." (xix) There is not loss of identity but the continuation of it. And our hope rests securely in the confidence that we were created to live, not to die. Our turning to God is an inward turning, one at the very depth of our nature.

> For this turning to the light and Spirit of God
> within thee is thy only true turning unto God; there
> is no other way of finding Him but in that place
> where He dwelleth in thee. For though God be every-
> where present, yet He is only present to thee in
> the deepest and most central part of thy soul. (x)

God is affirmed, intuitively grasped, or his nature revealed to us. We are not dealing with proofs of God's existence, expecting that belief in life after death comes in orderly fashion. Though some might argue to the contrary, it seems reasonably clear that there can be little security in belief about life after death without a strong theism. This God that we affirm is not proven as much as revealed and is grasped by intuitive insight. God is not a being among other beings. "We are, the world is, God is Being-Itself." (xi)

We do concur with Cyril Alington, one-time Dean of Durham: "The character of God must be the determining factor." So he continues with an affirmation that combines this with a conviction about life after death.

> ...if it be agreed that any intelligible universe
> must serve a moral purpose, it would seem to follow
> that, should 'personalities' be allowed to perish
> with those souls unmade the making of which seems
> to be its object, it is extremely difficult to
> justify, before the court of reason, the existence
> of our world at all. (xii)

It becomes very difficult, if not impossible, to believe in life after death without some dualistic approach to our natures. The differences in approaches to dualism are so vast that one may only point to the reams of pages written on this. At least we are here not concerned over establishing the existence of a distinct entity. We may only say that the problems about the existence of a separate soul (or its non-existence) seem endless. We noted earlier how even those who argue against the existence of a separate soul (D.Z. Phillips, for example) do have a form of dualism insofar as they maintain that there is any hope of life after death. Phillips does this at one place in terms of eternal life as participating in the life of God and in another place, as seeing us "known to God." (xiii) Certainly Phillips is not meaning here that we would survive death "in any empirical way such that what we now call life would go on.... Talk about eternal life is not dependent upon these assumptions." (Dr. Phillips wrote this in a letter to me clarifying why he wrote the monograph "Death and Immortality.") If, on one hand, death is a real event and the body ceases its functions, and on the other hand we insist that there is some form of life after death, then one is forced to believe in some kind of dualism. If we say that we participate in the life and love of God and that this continues, it is also obvious that the body we have known does not so continue. The biological life ceases. "Dust to dust."

What we are saying is that even when a strict dualism of body and soul is rejected or at least not adopted some form of dualism remains in most cases when there is belief in life after death. Hywel Lewis is helpful when he replies to those who say that a body (and space) of some kind is necessary.

> But suppose someone says: 'I agree, but surely you will need a body of some kind.' I do not think I would concede this, at least as an absolute requirement. But if the point were conceded, it would still mean that my continued existence was independent of any particular body that I might have at one stage. The body is replaceable while I remain the same. This commits us to dualism at least to the extent of making my own existence, in essentials, independent of my having a particular body, and especially my present physical body which, I have no doubt, will come to its end with the end of my 'allotted span.' (xiv)

Dr. Lewis is here replying in part to an article by Professor Sydney Shoemaker of Cornell University. This statement of Hywel Lewis indicates that life after death is not contingent upon preservation of this body. He also indicates that we may assume the "I" that remains, and know what it is without having to attempt a proof of a disembodied soul. We would insist that it is not possible to make a precise determination of what which continues. It may well be beyond our "ken" and have to be left to the world of mystery. But we may affirm with Lewis that it is possible for the essential "I" to continue.

There are times when what is meant by "spiritual body" is very close to the meaning that is conveyed by "soul." But the phrase "spiritual body" does carry special implications. Along with implying some functions of memory, will and identity there is implied a continuity of personality traits. Here the word "body" carries these more fully than the word "soul" usually does. And since this is a "spiritual body," the apostle Paul, and others, have insisted that this is not a new physical body. It seems reasonably clear that he is not making the case for a new body that requires space. It is a spiritual body, spiritual as God is Spirit and we certainly do not think of God as requiring space. What we do see as important is that our real being continues. In this we may have faith and confidence without having to have strict proofs. Actually, there are other thinkers who are more content with the "leap of faith" and who rest their confidence in faith in the God who, having created us, would not want our demise. D.Z. Phillips expresses this well:

> It is only when a man has become absorbed by the love of God that he ceases to ask such questions about vindication and rights not because he is sure of his profit, but because profit has nothing to do with the character of his love. The immortality of the soul has to do, not with...and the consequences...but with participation in God's life, in his contemplation of divine love.... The immortality of the soul refers to the state an individual is in in relation to the unchanging reality of God. (xv)

The Pauline phrase, "spiritual body," may fail logically and still be at the heart of the truth. It is possible on the one hand to fail to see the necessity for rigid logical arguments for all matters we deem important and on the other hand, to find rich meaning in this strange phrase "spiritual body." The Pauline approach grew out of a Judaistic emphasis on the oneness of a person's nature. So Paul's phrase "spiritual body" tries to convey something more than the concept of a soul. Most of the biblical tradition does not seek to prove the existence of a separate, substantial soul. Instead, the hope that arises out of New Testament thought is that we have, as a vital "part" of us, a spirit, a light that may live eternally, that which Helmut Thielicke calls "man's irreplaceable personhood." It would have identity for this is possibly what Paul was struggling to say in a day when he had no adequate word. "Spiritual body" may be inadequate for the word "body" carries too many implications that at times seem to counter "spirit." All we were saying here is that the New Testament hope does not rest in empirical proofs for the existence of a soul.

It is one of the handicaps of the word "soul" that it at times seems to conjure up an image of a disembodied spirit and does not have the full connotations of our personality. Paul's answer to use the phrase "spiritual body" also has its shortcomings but we see its direction as helpful. We see that he is saying as strongly as he can that what lives after death may be more of a full person than a disembodied spirit. Those heavily concerned over identity problems in our day may not be entirely satisfied with some of the beliefs projected here, but we are convinced that they have biblical roots and that they are reasonable.

When we speak then of our essence continuing, our real being living eternally, we are asserting that an identifiable George or Betty or Axel goes on. It is far from the ideal world of Plato. The apostle Paul speaks out of an Hebraic background that sees persons in totality. In moving to a new position, for him, affirming eternal life, Paul is trying to continue this view of oneness. The flesh must go in the act of death and die, but our spiritual being continues when we participate in eternal life. Hence the beauty of his imagery about the seed helps us as long as we do not carry it beyond the world of analogy and use it as a solid "proof."

It is important to point out that in the Gospel of John we find many references to eternal life but no mention of "our soul" attaining eternal life. Oscar Cullman in his Ingersoll lecture accentuates what we are trying to say at this point:

> Belief in the immortality of the soul is not belief in a revolutionary event. Immortality, in fact, is only a <u>negative</u> assertion: the soul does <u>not</u> die, but simply lives on. Resurrection is a <u>positive</u> assertion: the whole man, who has really died, is recalled to life by a new act of creation by God. Something has happened--a miracle of creation!... The whole Johannine Gospel emphasizes the point. We are already in the sate of resurrection, that of eternal life--not immortality of soul; the new era is already inaugurated. (xvi)

This may become clearer if we cite some representative Johannine passages on eternal life. The hope is there, but there are no meticulous proofs. And there is no mention of "soul."

> ...so that everyone who has faith in Him may possess eternal life. (3:15)
>
> God loved the world so much that He gave His only Son that everyone who has faith in Him may not die but have eternal life. (3:16)
>
> He who puts his faith in the Son has hold of eternal life. (3:36)
>
> The water that I shall give him will be an inner spring always welling up for eternal life. (4:14)
>
> The reaper is drawing his pay and gathering a cup for eternal life. (4:36)

> In very truth, anyone who gives heed to what I say and puts his trust in Him who sent me has hold of eternal life... (5:24)
>
> You must work, not for this perishable food, but for the food that lasts, the food of eternal life. (6:27)
>
> In truth, in very truth I tell you, the believer possesses eternal life. I am the bread of life. (6:47)
>
> My own sheep listen to my voice; I know them and they follow me. I give them eternal life and they shall never perish. (10:28)
>
> I know that His commands are eternal life. (12:50)
>
> ...For Thou has made him sovereign over all mankind, to give eternal life to all whom Thou has given him. This is eternal life: to know Thee who alone art truly God, and Jesus Christ whom Thou hast sent. (17:2,3)

At this point we are indicating that none of the writers we have surveyed (and they are persons of considerable ability) sees the necessity to prove the existence of a separate entity called soul. It is not the thrust of biblical literature either. The word is used, sometimes in the way that D.Z. Phillips indicates that it is used commonly--to speak of the kind of life we are living. And there is the strong conviction that a central dimension of our lives has eternal quality, or may possess it. We are not in any way denying that there is a dimension of our life that is divine; in fact, we would strongly maintain this. But this is not to attempt to <u>prove</u> beyond all doubt, through analytical reasoning, that there is a separate soul. We are therefore stressing that our center for belief in life after death does not come from proving the existence of the soul or its immortality but rather from an affirmation of eternal life.

Again, one must admit that there are variants on the resurrection concept. One could cite writers who firmly believe in the resurrection of the physical body. Some customs about the preservation of the corpse may stem from this view. Others think of resurrection as an event to happen in a future age. And we must differentiate the resurrection of Jesus Christ from our resurrection though our resurrection becomes possible only through Christ. Oscar Cullman does at points embrace some particular eschatological ideas (some of which are also clearly present in the New Testament) but he has presented a clear position that speaks of the resurrection, not the resurrection of the physical corpse. And this differentiation is quite helpful.

> ...in spite of the fact that the Holy Spirit is already so powerfully at work, men still die; even after Easter and Pentecost men continue to die as before. Our body remains mortal and subject to sickness...Instead of the fleshly matter there appears the spiritual. That is, <u>instead of corruptible matter there appears the incorruptible</u>. The visible and the invisible will be spirit. But let us make no mistake: this is certainly not the Greek sense of bodiless Ideas! A new heaven and a new earth! That is the Christian hope...our bodies also rise from the dead. Yet not as fleshly bodies, but as spiritual bodies.
>
> The expression which stands in the ancient texts of the Apostles' Creed is quite certainly not biblical: 'I believe in the resurrection of the flesh!' Paul could not say that. Flesh and blood cannot inherit the Kingdom. Paul believes in the resurrection of the <u>body</u>, not of the <u>flesh</u>. (xvii)

What is said here then is quite in line with the message of Paul himself:

> But you may ask, how are the dead raised? In what kind of body? How foolish! The seed you sow does

> not come to life unless it has first died; and what you sow is not the body that shall be, but a naked grain...and God clothes it.... As we have worn the likeness of the man made of dust, so we shall wear the likeness of the heavenly man. What I mean, my brothers, is this: flesh and blood can never possess the kingdom of God. (xviii)

This affirmation is tied up with our affirmation of God as Being-itself and with a divine aspect to our natures. It is possible to say that when we speak of this persistent aspect of our being we are really writing of the soul and not using the word. The word itself may be helpful at points, but the difference in our approach is that we are not seeking to prove the existence of the soul. We are affirming that in the light of our concept of a loving God who created us, and in the light of our belief that our natures are not only sinful but also divine, this aspect of ourselves may continue in eternal life through the grace of God. Just what this "aspect" is may always be a mystery. There is that as a part of our nature which is not wiped out when our bodies cease to function. Insofar as we are able to project it, there is some measure of identity and memory but this cannot be tied to brain functions. Jesus responded in affirmation to the thief on an adjacent cross: "To-day thou shalt be with me in paradise."

This spirit of affirmation, in place of meticulous argument, is found in many who deal with ideas about eternity. Huston Smith has an especially fine paragraph in his book "Forgotten Truth":

> At death man is ushered into the unimaginable expanse of a reality no longer fragmentary but total. Its all-revealing light shows up his earthly career for what it truly was, and the revelation comes at first as judgment.... And because the self is now identified with its Mind or vital center...Mind's larger norms, to which the embodied ego paid little

more than lip service, now hold the balance....and the self...passes to the Soul's immortal center, which is now freed for the beatific vision. Lost in continual adoration and wonder it abides in the direct presence of the Living God who is Being Itself. Beyond this, where the film that separates knower from known is itself removed and the self sinks into the Spirit that *is* the Infinite.... Ah, but we can say no more. We have reached the Cloud of Unknowing where the rest is silence. (xix)

In his book "Christian Hope," Dr. John MacQuarrie affirms that:

...as a Christian theologian, I would have to add that my hope that human beings have an eternal destiny does not rest on ingenious theories about a life 'after' death or 'beyond' death. We remind ourselves that we have simply been trying to show that such hopes are possible and cannot be dismissed as nonsense or lacking any rational defense...if God is indeed the God of love revealed in Jesus Christ, then death will not wipe out his care for the persons he has created. (xx)

We should, then, reexamine once more some of the meaning of the central Pauline passages. Margaret E. Thrall, lecturer in Bangor, surmises that Paul may have been trying to react against some Platonic ideas of immortality held by some Corinthians. But his response was also very probably colored by Pharisaic training in which Paul would have come to believe in some kind of resurrection view. He had no doubt pondered this for a long time, even before he became a Christian himself. Margaret Thrall's central comment gives solid conviction to the place of Christ in Paul's views. Christ brought a new day, a new possibility of relationship, so through His resurrection, our eternity gives us new hope. "Through his life, death, and resurrection," she writes, "he has brought into being a new kind of human existence, life which is wholly controlled by the Spirit of God and so is imperishable and eternal." (xxi)

One of the intriguing notes that keeps recurring in discussing the Pauline passage is that though the ear of corn looks different from the seed, the kernels in the ear look like the seed. A change has occurred but there is continuity. The new ear of corn is an ear of corn but not a head of lettuce. So the analogy would go that after death there would be a continuation of life that would have identifiable continuity with the life before death but it would be a new life. It would be the same and yet somewhat also not the same. An analogy is never proof but it does clarify an idea and it performs this function here. Margaret Thrall adds four important observations of value to us here. We summarize them thus:

> (i) We should not necessarily expect to know in detail what the life of the resurrection will be like (the question is a <u>senseless</u> one). No one who looks at a grain of wheat or any other seed can possibly tell from its external appearance what the plant will look like when it is grown....
> (ii) Since the plant differs from the seed in appearance we are not to suppose, like some of the Jews, that belief in the resurrection requires us to believe in the restoration of the material body with all its previous characteristics.
> (iii) The resurrection existence will be far more glorious than our present life, just as the plant is much more impressive and beautiful than the seed.
> (iv) There is continuity of some kind between our present life and the life of the resurrection. The seed and the plant are the same organism at different stages of its life-history. We shall be the same people, not different personalities entirely, when we are raised from the dead...

> When Paul talks of a <u>spiritual body</u> as the form our future existence will take we must...note that the word <u>body</u> is of considerable importance. We shall not be just disembodied spirits, little more than ghosts. We shall possess some bodily form for the expression of our personalities. (xxii)

(The last phrase is perhaps one that needs interpretation, but certainly in the light of other comments she makes, she is not thinking of a "bodily form" that is physical.) The affirmation is that one will continue, in some continuous life growing out of this one, that the new life will be more glorious but that specifics cannot be given about the range of our identity or the new world in which we will find ourselves. "We shall all be changed." "Now we see through a glass darkly" yet we may still have faith and hope.

We are affirming that the Spirit grasps the personal center and one then becomes engaged in "an experience of the presence of the infinite in the finite" (to use Tillich's words). We would continue then (again quoting Tillich) by affirming that everything, which includes each of us, "as created is rooted in the eternal ground of being." There is the other side to our lives, the fallen one, our desire to live the life of the prodigal. But to consider one side without the other is unrealistic. If we dwell only on our fallen nature without seeing the possibility of our participation in being is to end up in despair. It is possible to see what we mean by essence or our spirit without ignoring the demonic aspects. Our essence is our inmost, central nature and since it is our being-ness it may also be our good-ness. The word "spirit" if carefully used may be a better word for our purposes. It comprises the enduring elements of that which makes one a personality. The essence of spirit stands for our potentiality. "It does not yet appear what we shall be."

Insofar as we may affirm these things, we may also differentiate between that which is eternal and that which is temporal or transitory. It is not a matter of empiricism or non-empiricism for the eternal is experienced; indeed it may be the most shaking and vital of our experiences. William Law relates the "essences" to this eternal reality and adds that this which is our essence is and was and shall be eternal.

> Essences...had an Eternal Reality before they were in, or became a distinct Soul, and therefore they must have the same Eternal Reality in it. It was the Eternal Breath of God before it came before it came into Man... (xxiii)

Rufus Jones says that eternal life "is the entrance upon an absolutely satisfying experience whether here or elsewhere, in which the soul has found itself joined indissolubly with its Object..." He later ties this up with the Fourth Gospel and adds his interpretation that eternal life as seen there:

> ...is rather a life of new dimensions, life forever opening out and pushing forward in the Godward direction. It is infinitely expansive...Instead of going on in a straight line like the rail of a track, life gathers depth and volume as a cone does when you go from its apex downward. (xxiv)

Cyril Alington adds a strong Johannine reference saying that "to know God is life eternal..." (xxv) We should note here (partly since we have used him before) that the title of his very helpful work is a traditional phrase from the creed: "the life everlasting." For him this does not mean a "lasting" life that has endurance, but rather he interprets this as life eternal. He uses the two phrases quite interchangeably throughout. He does point out at one point that:

> St. John's definition of 'eternal life' is simply that it consists in 'knowing God': this definition finds a place in more than one of our Collects; we are daily reminded that 'in knowledge of God standeth our eternal life,' and the Collect for St. Philip and St. James' day declares that 'truly to know Him is everlasting life.' (xxvi)

As we are presenting this, eternal life then is not another dimension of time but is a different dimension of one's life. Berdyaev deals with this in strong fashion and consistently relates it to his views of paradise and hell.

> The ecstasy of creative inspiration, of love, of contemplating the divine light, transfers us for a moment to heaven, and those moments are no longer in time. Eternity is not a cessation of movement and of creative life; it is creative life of a different order, it is movement which is not spatial and temporal but inward. (xxxvi)

This is an important concept in Paul's thinking; he makes it clear that eternal life *is*, or at least may be. It is not a "coming," a future state, but it may possess us now. If it does, we shall remain in it--even after death. We see that as a central belief we may possess eternal life now--through the risen Christ. Meaningful prayer is independent upon this, for we are not just "children of time" as with some other creatures and not able to ask the questions of meaning. "Eternal life is life in the eternal, life in God." (xxviii) It is the key to the awareness of "presence" which Dr. Tillich says our age has lost the courage to accept and so we may have "lost the dimension of the eternal." (xxix) For the apostle Paul, eternal life is the new life in the Spirit, a life of surrender and agape, in contrast to the life of "natural man" with self-centeredness and a retaliatory life pattern. It is much as John's Gospel portrays this. In eternal life, we are fully the bearer of being. We have opened the door to participation in the life of Being Itself--our oneness with God.

We quite agree with Cyril Alington that the emphasis on eternal life does not conflict with belief in the resurrection but may well give it rich meaning. He quotes Bishop Westcott in his note on John vi.45:

> So far from the doctrine of the Resurrection being,

> as has been asserted, inconsistent with St. John's
> teaching on the present reality of eternal life,
> it would rather be true to say that this doctrine
> makes the necessity of the Resurrection obvious.
> He who feels that life <u>is</u> now, must feel that after
> death all that belongs to the essence of its present
> perfection must be restored, however much ennobled
> under new conditions of manifestation. (xxx)

The avenue by which we find this unity is through <u>participation</u> in the Being of God. This is a rich word. We do not stand apart then, but we overcome our separateness enough to participate in the depths of eternity. It is echoed in the posthumous writings of David Roberts, one-time Dean of Union Theological Seminary in New York City.

> Participation in the reality for which one sacrifices
> himself means that the significance and worth of
> personality-and-community are indestructible; for
> Being is indestructible. (xxxi)

This is the path by which the divine spirit of our very salves is in the Eternal Now. It is a sense of presence where we become in communion with the divine. It is Marcel who says that in this we find hope:

> It is a <u>presence</u> which evokes hope, not a cumulation
> of probabilities. Borne up by a communion whose
> very atmosphere is eternal, unreservedly disponible
> to the Absolute Presence which enfolds this
> communion, the soul moves ceaselessly beyond the
> reach of critical thought; and this movement reveals
> the intelligible core of hope. (xxxii)

One must ask more profound questions first. If eternal life is a way that our essence participates in Being Itself, then this may well be an ongoing, never-ending process, for Being Itself never ends. Many of our struggles would then cease. "He will wipe away every tear from their eyes; there shall be an end to death, and no mourning and crying and pain; for the old order has passed away.... There shall be no more night, nor will they need the light of lamp or sun, for the Lord God will give them light...." (xxxiv)

And when we confront the tragedy of a life cut off in early years or in what we might call "the prime of life" then we see the hope that this life may yet develop. This is why the concept of essentialization becomes an important one. That which continues is, in Paul's terminology, "the spiritual body." Few phrases to interpret this meaning seem better than one from Paul Tillich; he refers to this as "the Spiritually transformed total personality." (xxv) For Tillich, the capital "S" has significance. Through the Spirit, the grace of God, not our own power, works the transformation. One can always wish for further expansions and delineation, but some questions realizing that we will know only when the veil is lifted. Hywel Lewis also finds these limitations and yet he gives a firm hope.

> The hope we have...is not a luxury, a secondary consideration to be investigated on its own account; it belongs to the essence of a Christian commitment.... The work and person of Christ must be taken in its fullness, but it seems to be unthinkable that it should not be thought to include, in explicit word and in implication, the affirmation of our abiding place at the heart of God's love. (xxxvi)

This may well be where we must end in our thinking, in an affirmation of faith and hope. "Now we see only puzzling reflections in a mirror, but then we shall see face to face. My knowledge now is partial; then it will be whole..." (xxxvii) In a negative way we affirm that life after death is not a continuation of the struggle for daily bread, "getting and spending." We no longer "lay waste our powers." Eternal life is life lived in the essence, life lived under the Reign of God. "The whole personality participates in Eternal Life. If we use the term 'essentialization,' we can say that man's psychological, spiritual, and social being is implied..." (xxxviii)

If we can divest purgatory from much of its popular meaning, this concept might add to our hope. In its best sense, the concept of purgatory affirms that, at death, all is not frozen, that there is still room for further essentialization.

Though we would not stress a revival of purgatory as a necessary belief, we would indicate that at its heart, it says that our future development may continue. If taken in the light of Tillich's "essentialization," this may bring new hope. In his discussion with Margaret Mead to which we referred in an earlier chapter, Tillich adds that "perhaps one should be satisfied with the answer that eternal life is life, and therefore not static but dynamic..." (xxxix) This runs quite in contradiction to Phillip's dark description for if one cannot will any longer, one might wonder how that person could respond to the prayers of another. Dr. MacQuarrie comes closer to the Tillich position and one in which we find merit—and hope. In his "Principles of Christian Theology" he says that:

> No individual existence that has been called out of nothing will utterly return to nothing, but will move nearer to the fulfillment of its potentialities... (xl)

In his latest book Dr. MacQuarrie adds some phrases that expand this thought. There he speaks of the picture that "is in terms of the purgation of souls and their growth in a commonwealth of life, in which they have deepening communion with God and with each other." (xli) He writes in another place how certainly God cannot change the factuality of the past, but that "though one cannot change the facts of the past, the value of these facts can be changed and often is changed." (xlii) And he adds: "What I mean is that it is no dead or frozen past that is present to God but a past which is itself being transformed as God brings about his consummation." (xliii)

If we affirm all this, then we might also say that hell then could be the existence—or life—after death that did not know this essence, this oneness with being, this participatory life in the spirit. It would be a hellish, unsettling struggle, an existence with little hope. Certainly this is what Berdyaev had in mind as he presented his views on paradise and hell. But even in some of these passages there is some idea that further movement is possible. If we are free, then Berdyaev is right in insisting that there must be a world to choose--namely a hell state as a possibility. There would have to be another state of being or else freedom is a deception and all would be predestined to live in paradise. But if there is some idea of a purgatory we would not need to say with Dante about hell: "Abandon all hope, ye who enter here."

The paradise that we envision then would not be in the future. We see difficulties in structuring any ideas of paradise in a time sequence, even modifying it to conform with new post-Einstein ideas of time and space as Dr. MacQuarrie tries to do. A future that is only a prolongation of time could well be a hellish state. The life beyond is the life for which we hope, eternal, not an extension of our life here. It just is, and there we would be delivered from the turmoil of birth and growth and pain and losses and sickness. We would be. It is a state of participation in the life of God, of knowing eternal life fully, not in a partial sense. It is a world where one no longer promises for promises are fulfilled.

This is the path then to which many of these thinkers have contributed. They have built into our thought new dimensions about life after death. We see that, as we look towards a life beyond the incidence of death, we do not face it alone. Indeed, self-seeking is possibly one of the surest ways to a hellish existence. "He who would save his life will lose it, and he who will lose his life for my sake and the gospels will save it." (xliv) Gabriel Marcel, becoming a Christian in mature life, saw the power of this. He drives home the point relentlessly that we do not live alone, but in intersubjectivity. So as we approach matters about life after death, we do this not with objective analysis and proofs about my existence but in the world of intersubjectivity. So we participate in the divine and so we find hope. We are involved in the thoughts and process as we consider the meaning of our own death. It is in relationship that it takes on a profound meaning. Part of our concept of paradise is the communion of saints. "For all the saints who from their labours rest..."

What must be done--to inherit eternal life--is to find ourselves lifted up by the Second Adam, brought into newness of life in the spirit of Christ Himself. Once again we bring ourselves to this:

> What this new regained Birth is, we are plainly told by St. Peter, that is a being born again...by the Word, that is, the eternal Word...Which Divine Word being only in the Soul as a Seed, is to restore by degrees the first Birth of the Word, or Son of God in the soul. (xlv)

It is the Eternal who brings us into this new dimension of being, who gives us eternal life both here and now and after the death of the flesh.

> Resurrection says mainly that the Kingdom of God includes all dimensions of being. The whole personality participates in Eternal Life. (xlvi)

This participation is again not just for me or the favored friends that I approve. It brings hope to some of the ones with least hope, as to the thief upon a cross on a lonely hill. Our essentialization continues and continues with others. We dare not condemn others to a world without hope; it is possible that all who are in some way created by God are given hope through Him.

> The question and answer are possible only if one understands essentialization or elevation of the positive into Eternal Life as a matter of universal participation; in the essence of the least actualized individual, the essences of other individuals and, indirectly, of all being are present. Whoever

condemns anyone to eternal death condemns himself, because his essence and that of the other cannot be absolutely separated. (xlvii)

It could be hell to be separated from those whom we love. So our seeking for a life beyond the event of death is also that we hope for this life for others. We dare not seek only our own salvation. This is what it is to be accepted by God. This is then the greatest gift of all--"the certainty of being accepted by God." (xlviii)

Our hope lies in the confidence that we in our essential selves are divine as well as human, that our being may participate in eternal life with God who is Being Itself. Created in love, we may one day be in Love always. And there shall be no more hatred and bitterness, no more self-seeking and accusations. We will be a realm of eternal peace. There will be no night there, for the Lord God gives light.

So we have come full circle back to a seventeenth-century thinker whose earthly life was less than four decades. His mystical insights still give us hope.

...the lively sense of His own goodness of Himself hath excited within it; those breathings and graspings after an eternal participation of Him are but the energy of His own breath within us; if He had had any mind to destroy it, He would never have shewn it such things as He hath done; He would not raise it up to such mounts of vision, to shew it all the glory of that heavenly Canaan, flowing with eternal and unbounded pleasures, and then precipitate it again into the deep and darkest abyss of death and non-entity. (xlix)

SUMMARY

We have been seeking a central affirmation as a ground for belief in life after death. We have said that this belief must begin with a concept of God. We find that the experience of Moses in "the backside of the desert" (as one called it) is a profound beginning. That was not a series of logical propositions, but the experience was not illogical or irrational. It was an experience of awareness. So many of us have lesser experiences of awareness almost daily. We may watch a bush burning but not consumed, or we may be hearing the incredible warbling of an English blackbird in the spring-time, or we stand rapt in the myriad colors of a lovely sunset. We feel the urge to take off our shoes for the place whereon we stand in holy ground. We speak not just of a nature mysticism but of the awareness of a Presence in the world of experience. We are speaking then of an experiential base that moves us to an awareness of Goodness and Beauty and Truth without anyone having to prove it to us. Worship is not based on a proof but upon awareness. So our central affirmation grows from an experience. As we stand in the presence of an amazing experience of holiness--with the stirring sound of a great organ, or hearing the rich beauty of the Welsh singing their hymns, or in stillness experience the beauty of centering down in a Friend's meeting, we are then participating in the reality of God; we are aware of His presence.

Beginning with this awareness, we slowly expanded our concept with biblical insights and from some insights found in writers centuries later. Again, many of these insights come from moments of great awareness, with the power of revelation at work. The Divine Spirit has been seeking to reveal itself and its nature. Insofar as we have been open to that Spirit there have been helpful insights.

If we assume that we were created by a loving God, then we could further assume that this Creator who loves us would want the essential part of our lives to continue. A wood carver holds his carving with care and bestows a measure of love on that which he has created.

It would hurt to see it destroyed. If a carver may do so with a future continuance for his creation out of wood, how much more might a divine Creator wish that His creations would live eternally? Or see how a parent loves his or her children. It is only reasonable to assume that if God is a God of love this God would wish only for our continuance, not for our destruction. Jesus' analogies about the birds of the air and the lilies of the field would only reinforce what we are saying.

If we can agree to this point, then we may assume that it is plausible to project life beyond the incident of death. On the one hand, for many persons, their creativity has not reached its peak and reaches out to continue beyond the incident of death that has come very soon for them. On the other hand, if God is good and a God of love, it does seem more logical to believe that this God of love would not want these amazing creatures to be destroyed. Even five score years is short in the timeless world of God. So we may have some confidence that this good God would make it possible for the persons that are loved to live eternally. John MacQuarrie expresses this in "Christian Hope" when he says that "if God is indeed the God of love revealed in Jesus Christ, then death will not wipe out his care for the persons he has created." (i)

If we have reached a level of participation in the New Being in Christ, then following death, this may involve a fuller participation in the life of the Spirit. If God is loving and forgiving, would not this God want each of us to reach a fuller life in the Spirit? Our hope then rests in our participation in the Eternal Now and the hope that evolves for eternal life. Our essential being--our "spiritual body,"--enters into eternal life as one moves through the portals of death. The new plant takes on new life, life that began in the world of struggle and day-by-day existence. The intimations from moments of oneness in the days and years of earthly life are part of the grounds for hope that in the eternity beyond death "there will be no more sea," no more separation. "Then we shall know even as we are now known."

FOOTNOTES

FOOTNOTES
Chapter I

(i)   Cullman, Oscar: In his Ingersoll lecture at Harvard University in 1955 published by Epworth Press, London, 1958 and reproduced in Terence Penelhum's anthology: "Immortality" published by Wadsworth Publishing Co., Belmont, California, 1973, p. 56.

FOOTNOTES
Chapter II

(i)	Job 14:7–15.
(ii)	Ibid., 26:5, 6.
(iii)	Ibid., 33:16–18.
(iv)	Ibid., 33:28–30.
(v)	Psalm 90:1, 2 (RSV).
(vi)	Psalm 121:8 (RSV).
(vii)	Psalm 23:14 (RSV).
(viii)	Psalm 1139:8–10 (RSV).
(ix)	Eichrodt, p. 526.
(x)	Hooke, p. ix.
(xi)	Nickelsburg, p. 88.
(xii)	Clarke, p. 11.
(xiii)	Ibid., p. 61.
(xiv)	W.S., 4:1.
(xv)	W.S., 3:7, 8.
(xvi)	Charles, Ps., Vol. II, p. 185.
(xvii)	I Enoch 5:1, 2.
(xviii)	Secrets of Enoch, 8:5–8.
(xix)	Charles, Ps., Vol. II, p. 479.
(xx)	2 Baruch, 30:3–5.
(xxi)	Charles, Ps., Vol. II, p. 508.
(xxii)	Ibid., p. 508.

FOOTNOTES
Chapter III

(i) Nucho, Fuad: "Berdyaev's Philosophy: The Existential Paradox of Freedom and Necessity," Doubleday, Garden City, New York, 1966, p. 22.
(ii) Davy, M.: "Nicolas Berdyaev: Man of the Eighth Day," Geoffrey Bles, London, 1967.
(iii) DR, p. 292.
(iv) TR, p. 12.
(v) DM, p. 351.
(vi) Steere, Douglas: "On Beginning From Within," Harpers, New York, 1943, p. 132ff.
(vii) cf. DM, p. 122.
(viii) DM, p. 258.
(ix) Ibid.
(x) Ibid.
(xi) Ibid.
(xii) DM, p. 261.
(xiii) DM, p. 262.
(xiv) Chapter VIII is entitled: "The Paradox of Evil. The Ethics of Hell and Anti-Hell, Reincarnation and Transfiguration."
(xv) DM, p. 267.
(xvi) Ibid.
(xvii) DM, p. 267.
(xviii) Ibid.
(xix) TR, p. 135.
(xx) DM, p. 276.
(xxi) DM, p. 277.
(xxii) Ibid.
(xxiii) Ibid.
(xxiv) DM, p. 278.

(xxv)	DM, p. 279.
(xxvi)	Ibid.
(xxvii)	DM, p. 281.
(xxviii)	Ibid.
(xxix)	DM, p. 282.
(xxx)	Ibid.
(xxxi)	S.S., p. 155.
(xxxii)	Ibid.
(xxxiii)	S.S., p. 154.
(xxxiv)	DM, p. 288.
(xxv)	DM, p. 298.
(xxvi)	DM, p. 292.
(xxxvii)	DM, p. 293.
(xxxviii)	DM, p. 295.
(xxxix)	MCA, p. 309.
(xl)	MCA, p. 297.
(xli)	MCA, p. 296.
(xlii)	FS, p. 239.
(xliii)	FS, pp. 240-241.
(xliv)	FS, p. 242.
(xlv)	FS, pp. 247, 248.
(xlvi)	Ibid.
(xlvii)	FS, p. 256.
(xlviii)	FS, p. 260.
(xlix)	Ibid.
(l)	FS, p. 265.
(li)	FS, p. 260.
(lii)	FS, p. 262.
(liii)	FS, p. 266.
(liv)	DR, pp. 322, 323.
(lv)	DM, p. 294.

FOOTNOTES
Chapter IV

(i)   E.B., p. 25.
(ii)   M.J., p. 133.
(iii)   P. & I., p. 236.
(iv)   Ibid., p. 237.
(v)   Ibid., p. 238.
(vi)   Ibid.
(vii)   Miceli, Vincent: "Ascent to Being," Desclee Co., New York, 1965, p. 7.
(viii)   P. & I., p. 24.
(ix)   P. & I., p. 29.
(x)   P. & I., p. 86.
(xi)   P. & I., p. 239.
(xii)   P. & I., p. 88.
(xiii)   P. & I., p. 18.
(xiv)   C.F., p. 145.
(xv)   MIHE, pp. 193, 194.
(xvi)   Ibid., pp. 97, 98.
(xvii)   Ibid., p. 146.
(xviii) P. & I., p. 88.
(xix)   Roberts, David, "Existentialism and Religious Belief," Oxford University Press, New York, 1957, p. 326.
(xx)   P. & I., p. 239.
(xxi)   P.F., p. 93.
(xxii)   H.V., p. 133.
(xxiii) M.B., II, p. 172.
(xxiv)   Ibid.
(xxv)   M.B., II, p. 175.
(xxvi)   M.B., II, p. 173.
(xxvii) Ibid.
(xxviii) M.B., II, p. 171

(xxix)	M.B., II, pp. 171, 172.
(xxx)	C.F., p. 99.
(xxxi)	MIHE, pp. 248, 249.
(xxxii)	M.B., II, pp. 173, 174.
(xxxiii)	M.B., II, p. 174.
(xxxiv)	M.B., II, p. 175.
(xxxv)	Ibid., p. 98.
(xxxvi)	Roberts, p. 326.
(xxxvii)	P. & I., p. 240.
(xxxviii)	Christopher Publishing, Boston, 1954.
(xxxix)	P. & I., p. 241.
(xl)	P. & I., p. 242.
(xli)	Roberts, pp. 326, 327.
(xlii)	M.B., II, p. 69.
(xliii)	Ibid.
(xliv)	M.B., II, p. 73.
(xlv)	M.B., II, p. 175.
(xlvi)	P.F., pp. 100, 101.
(xlvii)	TWB, p. 138.
(xlviii)	M.B., II, p. 179.
(xlix)	Ibid.
(l)	P. & I., p. 232.
(li)	P. & I., p. 231.
(lii)	Gallagher, Kenneth I.: "The Philosophy of Gabriel Marcel," Fordham University Press, New York, 1962, p. 77.
(liii)	Ibid., pp. 77, 78.
(liv)	M.B., II, p. 168.
(lv)	MIHE, p. 75.
(lvi)	Gallagher, op.cit., p. 78.
(lvii)	Ibid., p. 70.
(lviii)	M.B., II, p. 198.
(lix)	Ibid., p. 182.
(lx)	Ibid.

FOOTNOTES
Chapter V

(i)	Hick, D.Z.E.H., p. 216.
(ii)	HDB, p. 2.
(iii)	HCT, p. xxv.
(iv)	Ibid., p. 136.
(v)	Ibid., p. 316.
(vi)	Ibid., p. 317.
(vii)	Ibid., p. 318.
(viii)	S.T., III, p. 242.
(ix)	S.T., II, p. 83.
(x)	Ibid., p. 84.
(xi)	Ibid., p. 177.
(xii)	HCT, p. 316.
(xiii)	May, p. 104.
(xiv)	S.T., I, p. 263.
(xv)	Ibid., p. 205.
(xvi)	S.T., III, p. 415.
(xvii)	S.T., I, p. 238.
(xviii)	S.T., III, pp. 420, 421.
(xix)	Ibid., p. 420.
(xx)	S.F., p. 172.
(xxi)	Cullman, Oscar: "Immortality of the Soul or Resurrection of the Dead?" Ingersoll lecture, Harvard, 1955. Reprinted in Penelhum, Terence: "Immortality," Wadsworth, Belmont, California, 1973, pp. 53ff.
(xxii)	S.T., III, p. 409.
(xxiii)	Ibid., p. 410.
(xxiv)	Ibid.
(xxv)	E.N., p. 125.
(xvi)	Ibid.
(xxvii)	Ibid., p. 131.

(xxviii)   Ibid.
(xxix)   Ibid., p. 132.
(xxx)   S.T., III, p. 410.
(xxxi)   Ibid., p. 412.
(xxxii)   S.T., I, p. 250.
(xxxiii)   S.T., III, p. 26.
(xxxiv)   Ibid., p. 29.
(xxv)   See B.T., I, pp. 236ff.
(xxxvi)   See Nels Ferre, ot.cit., p. 16.
(xxxvii)   S.T., III, p. 21.
(xxxviii)   Ibid., p. 24.
(xxxix)   E.N., p. 84.
(xl)   Ibid., p. 26.
(xli)   Ibid., p. 28.
(xlii)   Ibid., see pp. 30-32ff.
(xliii)   Ibid., p. 412.
(xliv)   Ibid.
(xlv)   Romans 8:5, 6 From the New English Bible translation,
              Oxford University Press, New York, 1970.
(xlvi)   S.T., III, p. 414.
(xlvii)   Luke 15:17.
(xlviii)   S.T., p. 204.
(xlix)   S.T., III, p. 406.
(l)   Ibid., p. 413.
(li)   S.T., I, p. 225.
(lii)   S.T., III, p. 410.
(liii)   Ibid., p. 413.
(liv)   Ibid.
(lv)   Ibid.
(lvi)   Ibid.
(lvii)   S.T., III, p. 414.
(lviii)   Ibid.
(lix)   Hammond, ot.cit., p. 104.

(lx)   Ibid.
(lxi)   Ibid.
(lxii)   S.T., III, p. 414.
(lxiii)   Ibid.
(lxiv)   Ibid.
(lxv)   I John 3:2 (New English Bible).
(lxvi)   S.T., III, p. 414.
(lxvii)   Ibid.
(lxviii)   Ibid., p. 408.
(lxix)   Ibid., p. 409.
(lxx)   Ibid.
(lxxi)   Ibid., p. 401.
(lxxii)   Ibid., p. 403.
(lxxiii)   Ibid.
(lxxiv)   Ibid., p. 417.
(lxxv)   Ibid.
(lxxvi)   I.M., pp. 23, 24.
(lxxvii)   S.T., III, p. 226.
(lxxviii)   Ibid., p. 222.
(lxxix)   Ibid.
(lxxx)   Ibid.
(lxxxi)   E.N., p. 123.
(lxxxii)   E.N., P. 125.
(lxxxiii)   S.T., III, p. 420.
(lxxxiv)   Ibid.
(lxxxv)   HDB, p. 2.
(lxxxvi)   Ibid.
(lxxxvii)   Ibid., p. 4.
(lxxxviii) Ibid.
(lxxxix)   Ibid.
(xc)   Ibid., p. 5.
(xci)   Ibid., p. 6.
(xcii)   Ibid., p. 7.

(xciii)   Ibid.
(xciv)   Ibid.
(xcv)   Ibid.
(xcvi)   Ibid.
(xcvii)   Ibid.
(xcviii)   Huston Smilth: "Human Fulfillment," in "The Search for America" (ed., by H. Smith), Prentice-Hall, Englewood Cliffs, 1959, pp. 173, 174.

FOOTNOTES
Chapter VI

(i)	C.H., p. 117.
(ii)	Becker, p. 285.
(iii)	Kung, Hans: "Eternal Life?", Doubleday, Garden City, New York, 1984, pp. 232, 233.
(iv)	Job 42:5 (RSV).
(v)	Rahner, Vol. VII, p. 13.
(vi)	Romans 8:9, 10 (NEB).
(vii)	HCT, p. 165.
(viii)	Unamuno, pp. 212, 213.
(ix)	John 1:1-5 (NEB).
(x)	Law, S.P., p. 28.
(xi)	S.T., p. 51.
(xii)	Alington, p. 28.
(xiii)	D. & I., p. 59. Second quote is from a letter written by Professor Phillips dated 3rd May, 1979.
(xiv)	Persons, p. 132.
(xv)	D. & I., pp. 38 and 55.
(xvi)	Cullman, pp. 27 and 35.
(xvii)	Ibid., pp. 45, 46.
(xviii)	I Corinthians 15:35-38, 49, 50 (NEB).
(xix)	Huston Smith, pp. 143, 144.
(xx)	C.H., p. 127.
(xxi)	Thrall, pp. 112, 113.
(xxii)	Ibid.
(xxiii)	Law, William, "Appeal," p. 64.
(xxiv)	Foundations, p. 27.
(xxv)	Alington, p. 67.
(xxvi)	Ibid., p. 65.
(xxvii)	Ibid., p. 298.
(xxviii)	S.T., III, p. 420.
(xxix)	E.N., p. 131.

(xxx)	Alington, p. 73.
(xxxi)	Roberts, David: "Existentialism and Religious Belief," Oxford University Press, New York, 1957, p. 326.
(xxxii)	Gallagher, Kenneth: "The Philosophy of Gabriel Marcel," Fordham University Press, New York, 1962, p. 77.
(xxxiii)	Revelations 22:5 (NEB).
(xxxiv)	Tillich, S.T., III, p. 412.
(xxxv)	Persons, p. 159.
(xxxvi)	I Corinthians 13:12 (NEB)
(xxxvii)	Tillich, S.T., III, p. 413.
(xxxviii)	Tillich, IM, pp. 23, 24.
(xxxix)	P.S.T., p. 361.
(xl)	C.H., p. 119.
(xli)	Ibid., p. 120.
(xlii)	Ibid.
(xliii)	Mark 8:35 (NEB).
(xliv)	Appeal, p. 81.
(xlv)	Tillich, S.T., III, p. 413.
(xlvi)	Ibid., p. 409.
(xlvii)	Ibid., p. 222.
(xlviii)	Smith, Discourses, pp. 103, 104.
(xlix)	C.H., p. 127.

FOOTNOTES
SUMMARY

(i) C.H., p. 127.

SELECTED BIBLIOGRAPHY
(with coding for footnotes)

Alington	Alington, Cyril: "The Life Everlasting," Basil Blackwell, Oxford, 1947.
	"The Apocrypha and Pseudepigrapha in English," edited by R.F. Charles, Oxford, Clarendon Press, 1913.
Badham	Badham, Paul: "Christian Beliefs About Life After Death," Macmillan, London, 1976.
	Badham, Paul: "The Relative Validity of Alternative Christian Beliefs About Life After Death, and the Ways in Which They Depend on Particular Theories of What It Means to be a Person." Doctoral thesis, 1973.
Becker	Becker, Ernest: "The Denial of Death," Free Press (Macmillan), New York, 1973.
DM	Berdyaev, Nicolas: "The Destiny of Man," Geoffrey Bles, London, 1955 (Torchbook edition): Harper Brothers, New York, 1960.
DR	Berdyaev, Nicolas: "Dream and Reality," Macmillan Company, New York, 1951.
FS	Berdyaev, Nicolas: "Freedom and the Spirit," Charles Scribner's Sons, New York, 1935.
MCA	Berdyaev, Nicolas: "The Meaning of the Creative Act," Harper & Brothers, New York, 1954 (first completed in 1914).
S.S.	Berdyaev, Nicolas: "Solitude and Society," Charles Scribner's Sons, New York, 1938.
TR	Berdyaev, Nicolas: "Truth and Revelation," Geoffrey Bles, London, 1953.
UF	Berdyaev, Nicolas: "Ungrund and Freedom," introductory essay in Boehme, Jacob: "Six Theosophic Points," University of Michigan Press, Ann Arbor, 1958.

Bewer	Bewer, Julius: "Literature of the Old Testament," Columbia University Press, New York, 1933.
Blackham	Blackham, H.J.: "Six Existentialist Thinkers," Macmillan, New York, 1952.
Bluck	Bluck, R.S.: "Plato's Phaedo," Routledge & Kegan Paul, Ltd., London, 1955.
Brehier	Brehier, Emile: "The Philosophy of Plotinus," translated by Joseph Thomas, University of Chicago Press, Chicago and London.
Bullett	Bullett, Gerald: "The English Mystics," Michael Joseph, London, 1950.
Carrington	Carrington, Hereward: "Mysterious Psychic Phenomena," Christopher Publishing House, Boston, 1954.
Cassirer	Cassirer, Ernst: "The Platonic Renaissance in England," translated by J.P. Pettegrove, University of Texas Press, Austin, Texas, 1953.
Charles	Charles, R.H.: "Eschatology: The Doctrine of a Future Life in Israel, Judaism and Christianity." Schocken, 1963, New York.
Church	Church, F.J.: "Phaedo" (translated by Church with introduction), Bobbs Merrill Co., Indianapolis, 1951.
Clarke	Clarke, Ernest G.: "The Wisdom of Solomon," Cambridge Commentary. Cambridge University Press, Cambridge, England, 1973.
Cullman	Cullman, Oscar: "Immortality of the Soul or Resurrection of the Dead?" Ingersoll lecture given at Harvard, Epworth Press, London, 1958.
Davy	Davy, Mlle. M.: "Nicolas Berdyaev: Man of the Eighth Day," Geoffrey Bles, London, 1967.
Eichrdot	Eichrdot, Walter: "Theology of the Old Testament," translated by J.A. Baker, SCM Press, Ltd., 1967.
Gallagher	Gallagher, Kenneth I.: "The Philosophy of Gabriel Marcel," Fordham University Press, New York, 1962.

Geach	Geach, Peter: "God and the Soul," Routledge and Kegan Paul, London, 1969.
Hall	Hall, Robert William: "Plato and the Individual," Martinus Nijhoff, The Hague, 1963.
Happold	Happold, F.C.: "Mysticism: A Study of an Anthology," Penguin Books, Harmondsworth, Middlesex, England, 1963.
Hepburn	Hepburn, Ronald: "Christianity and Paradox," Watts, London, 1958.
Hick	Hick, John: "Death and Eternal Life," Harper & Row, New York, 1977.
Hocking	Hocking, William Ernest: "The Meaning of Immortality in Human Experience," Harper, New York, 1957.
Horton	Horton, Walter Marshall: "Christian Theology," 1956.
Hooke	Hooke, S.H.: "The Resurrection of Christ as History and Experience." Darton, Longman and Todd, London, 1967.
Hunter	Hunter, A.M.: "The Gospel According to John" (Cambridge Bible Commentary), Cambridge University Press, Cambridge, 1965.
Inge	Inge, William Ralph: "The Philosophy of Plotinus," in two volumes. Third edition, originally printed in 1929, Longman's, Green & Co., Ltd.
FM	Jones, Rufus, M.: "Flowering of Mysticism, The Friends of God in the Fourteenth Century," Macmillan, New York, 1939.
NQ	"The New Quest," Macmillan & Co., Ltd., London, 1928.
NSMR	"New Studies in Mystical Religion" (The Ely lectures at Union Theological Seminary, New York), Macmillan, Ltd., London, 1928.
RL	"The Radiant Life" (including "The Spell of Immortality," the Ingersoll lecture at Harvard), Macmillan, New york, 1945.

RF	"Religious Foundations" (Anthology edited by Jones including a chapter of his own), Macmillan, New York, 1923.
SM	"Spirit in Man," Peacock Press, Berkeley, California, 1963.
SMR	"Studies in Mystical Religion" (first edition: 1909), Macmillan, Ltd., London, 1923.
Kung	Kung, Hans: "Eternal Life?" translated by Edward Quinn, Doubleday & Co., Garden City, New York, 1984.
Appeal	Law, William: "Appeal to All Who Doubt," London, 1740, printed for W. Innys and J. Richardson.
SP	Law, William: "Spirit of Prayer," edited by Sidney Spencer, James Clarke & Co., Ltd., Cambridge, 1967.
Lewis	Lewis, Hywel: "Persons and Life After Death," Macmillan, Ltd., London, 1978.
S & I	Lewis, Hywel: "The Self and Immortality," Macmillan, London, 1973.
CH	MacQuarrie, John: "Christian Hope," Seabury Press, New York, 1978.
Humility	MacQuarrie, John: "Humility of God," SCM Press, Ltd., London, 1978.
GT	MacQuarrie, John: "God Talk," SCM Press, London, 1967.
PCT	MacQuarrie, John: "Principles of Chrisstian Theology," Charles Scribner's, New York, 1971.
B.H.	Marcel, Gabriel: "Being and Having," A. & C. Black (Dacre Press), Great Britain, 1949, Collins, Fontana Library, 1965.
E.B.	Marcel, Gabriel: "The Existential Background of Human Dignity," Harvard University Press, Cambridge, Mass., 1963.

C.F.	Marcel, Gabriel: "Creative Fidelity," Noonday Press, New York, 1964.
H.V.	Marcel, Gabriel: "Homo Viator," Harper & Row, New York, 1962. Also published in 1951 by Victor Gollancz, London, and Henry Regnery Co., Chicago, 1951.
M.M.S.	Marcel, Gabriel: "Man Against Mass Society," Henry Regnery Co., Chicago, 1962.
M.J.	Marcel Gabriel: "Metaphysical Journal" Henry Regnery Co., Chicago, 1952. (Translated by Bernard Wall.)
M.B.I.	Marcel, Gabriel: "The Mystery of Being, Reflection and Mystery," Vol. I, Harvill Press, Ltd., Great Britain, 1950 and Henry Regnery Co., Chicago, 1960 (English translation by G.S. Fraser).
M.B. II	Marcel, Gabriel: "The Mystery of Being, Faith and Reality," Vol. II, Harvill Press, Ltd., Great Britain, 1951, Henry Regnery, Chicago, 1960. (Translated by Rene Hague.)
P.F.	Marcel, Gabriel: "Philosophical Fragments: 1909-1914." University of Notre Dame Press, Notre Dame, Indiana, 1965.
P.E.	Marcel, Gabriel: "The Philosophy of Existence" (translated by Manya Harari). Books for Libraries Press, Freeport, New York, 1969.
P & I	Marcel, Gabriel: "Presence and Immortality" (translated by Michael A. Machado), Duquesne University Press, Pittsburgh, Pennsylvania, 1967.
P.M.	Marcel, Gabriel: "Problematic Man" (translated by Brian Thompson), Herder and Herder, New York, 1967.
R.M.	Marcel, Gabriel: "Royce's Metaphysics" (translated by Virginia and Gordon Ringer), Henry Regnery Co., Chicago, 1956.

T.P.	Marcel, Gabriel: "Three Plays," Hill and Wang, New York, 1965.
TW&B	Marcel, Gabriel: "Tragic Wisdom and Beyond" (including conversations between Paul Ricoeur and Gabriel Marcel). Northwestern University Press, Evanston, 1973.
A.B.	Miceli, Vincent, S.J.: "Ascent to Being," Desclee Co., New York, 1965.
Nucho	Nucho, Fuad: "Berdyaev's Philosophy: The Existential Paradox of Freedom and Necessity," with introduction by Richard Kroner, Doubleday and Company, Garden City, New York, 1966.
Ornstein	Ornstein, Robert: "Psychology of Consciousness," Second Edition, Harcourt, Brace, Jovanovich, New York, 1977.
Owen	Owen, H.P.: "Concepts of Deity," Macmillan, London, 1971.
B.Q.T.	Pannenberg, Wolfhart: "Basic Questions in Theology," SCM Press, London, 1967.
F.R.	Pannenburg, Wolfhart: "Faith and Reality," Westminster Press, Philadelphia, 1977.
Patterson	Patterson, Robert Leet: "Plato on Immortality," Pennsylvania State University Press, 1965.
Penelhum	Penelhum, Terence: "Immortality," Wadsworth, Belmont, California, 1973.
D & I	Phillips, D.Z.: "Death and Immortality," Macmillan, London, 1970.
R & U	Phillips, D.Z. (editor): "Religion and Understanding," Basil Blackwell, Oxford, 1967.
R.W.P.	Phillips, D.Z.: "Religion Without Explanation" Basil Blackwell, Oxford, 1977.
Pieper	Pieper, Josef: "Death and Immortality," Burns & Oates, London, 1969.

Plotinus	Plotinus: "The Enneads," translated by Stephen MacKenna, third edition, Pantheon Books, Inc., New York.
E.P.R.	Price, H.H.: "Essays in the Philosophy of Religion," Clarendon Press, Oxford, 1972.
S&IAW	Price, H.H.: "Survival and the Idea of Another World." Lecture given at the Society for Psychical Research; see the Society's <u>Proceedings</u>, Volume 50, part 182, January 1953.
Rahner	Rahner, Karl: "Theological Investigations," Darton, Longman's and Todd, London, 1967.
Roberts	Roberts, David: "Existentialism and Religious Belief," Oxford University Press, New York, 1957.
Rowley	Rowley, H.H.: "From Moses to Qumram," Lutterworth Press, 1963.
Smith	Smith, Huston: "Forgotten Truth," Harper & Row, New York, 1977.
H.F.	Smith, Huston: "Human Fulfillment" in "Search for America," Prentice Hall, New Jersey, 1959.
Spencer	Spencer, Sidney: "Mysticism in World Religions," George Allen and Unwin, Ltd., London, 1961.
OBW	Steere, Douglas: On Beginning From Within." Harper & Row Bros., New York and London, 1943 (including his Ingersoll lecture). Personnel correspondence.
Van Ewijk	Van Ewijk, Thomas, J.M.: "Gabriel Marcel," Paulist Press, Glen Rock, New Jersey, 1965.
Vining	Vining, Elizabeth Gray: "Friend of Life: The Biography of Rufus M. Jones," J.P. Lippincott Co., Philadelphia, 1958.
Whale	Whale, John S.: "Christian Doctrine," Cambridge, England, at the University Press, 1941.
Taylor	Taylor, A.E.: "The Christian Hope of Immortality," Geoffrey Bles, London, 1938.

EN	Tillich, Paul: "The Eternal Now," Charles Scribner's Sons, New York, 1963.
HCT	Tillich, Paul: "History of Christian Thought," edited by Carl E. Braaten, Simon & Schuster, 1967, 1968.
IM	Tillich, Paul: "The Immortality of Man," article in "Pastoral Psychology," Vol. III, No. 75 for June 1975.
S.E.L.	Tillich, Paul: "Symbols of Eternal Life," Ingersoll lecture for 1962, Harvard University Bulletin 26, No. 3, April 1962.
ST	Tillich, Paul: "Systematic Theology," University of Chicago Press, Vol. I, 1951, Vol. II, 1957, Vol. III, 1963.
Threthowan	Threthowan, Illtyd: "Mysticism and Theology," Geoffrey Chapman, 1975.
Unamuno	Unamuno, Miguel de: "Agony of Christianity," Routledge and Kegan Paul, London, 1974.
G & G	Weil, Simone: "Gravity and Grace," Routledge and Kegan Paul, London, 1963.
WG	Weil, Simone: "Waiting on God," Fontana, 1959.

PAUL TILLICH

Symbols of Eternal Life

The Ingersoll Lecture 1962

Reprinted from *The Harvard Divinity Bulletin*, Vol. 26, No. 3, April 1962

I. Man's experience of the eternal as the source of the symbols of eternal life.

Everything in the universe is subject to the temporal process, which means not having been before and, after a definite span of time, ceasing to be. The awareness of this situation is called anxiety and it exists in all beings in whom the dimension of self-awareness is actual. Basic anxiety and awareness of finitude are identical.

Man is not only anxiously aware of his finitude; he also recognizes its implications. He anticipates his future non-being and he knows that once he was not. But in knowing this about himself and his world he is at the same time above both. He participates in a universal truth which as truth is not subject to temporality. The meaning of time itself is not temporal.

The act of knowing is only one of the acts of the human spirit which are transtemporal: the experience of the moral imperative and its unconditional character, despite changes of content and mode of expression, of the ideas of justice and humanity, of the unconditional concern about life, the experience of the holy — all have within their temporal aspect an element of transtemporality or eternity.

Expressions of this experience have existed since the infancy of mankind. Belief in the spirits of the dead, either venerated, as in China, or banished into the underworld, as in Greece, presupposes the idea of a mortal and an immortal part in man, while the conception of immortal beings — the gods — and those who by reason of their virtue attain to immortality, as certain heroes in Greece and the martyrs in later Judaism, attributes the element of eternity to divine or exalted human figures. But only in the post-polytheistic development of religion did the idea of eternal life become a religious problem eliciting different answers to the question of what evidence may exist for such a belief.

First, I want to give a sharper formulation of the idea by circumscribing the concept of eternity. Its origin was probably a vision, based on the experience of the unity of time in memory and anticipation. The divine spectator of this unity overlooks large stretches of time and finally all time. This is implied in the Hebrew idea of *olam* (in the plural *olamim haolamim*, eternities of eternities; in Greek, αἰῶνες αἰώνων; in Latin, *aeternitates aeternitatum*). It is the idea of the unity of a long, but still limited, time. It is not timelessness. The latter is experienced, e.g., in the timeless validity of a mathematical proposition, sometimes defined as the simultaneous presence of everything. The genuine concept of eternity is not timeless simultaneity; eternity is rather the transtemporal unity of the consecutive moments of temporality. This implies the rejection of the opposite distortion of eternity: its identification with endless temporality. Endlessness is the prolongation of time without limit, but it is not eternity; as Hegel has it, it is "bad infinity." Good infinity is eternity. Despite his belonging to the order of temporality, man belongs likewise to the order of eternity.

The oldest and everpresent answer to the question of the evidence for man's participation in eternity is the identity of the deepest Ground in man with the deepest Ground of reality. The classical Indian formulation of it is the identity of Atman with Brahman. The Ground of Universal Being is present in the Ground of our being. In recognizing this identity we recognize the double relation of man to the world of seeming reality in which we live in time and space, and to its Ground, out of which everything comes and to which all must return — ultimate reality. Similar in Western thought is Plotinus' formulation: If the soul is in the divine One, "she is not in something else, but in herself." And conversely: If the soul is with herself alone, separated from everything that is, she is in the One, the divine, the ultimate reality. In order to have this experience, man must empty himself of the contents of his empirical consciousness.

One may call this the mystical experience, if the word mystical is kept free from such distorting connotations as foggy, irrational, emotional, etc., which have made the word almost useless; but we need an abbreviation for the way in which countless billions of people in the history of mankind, especially in the East, have experienced the ultimate meaning of life. So let us keep the word mystical. Certainly this evidence is not based on a theoretical argument for our claims to eternity. We discover eternity to the degree in which we discover the Ground of all being within ourselves.

The opposite religious type is usually called the prophetic one. The discussion about the eternal destiny of man in later Judaism, in which Jesus participated, brought forth from him the great words: "Have ye not read what was spoken unto you by God, saying, 'I am the God of Abraham and the God of Isaac and the God of Jacob.' God is not the God of the dead, but of the living." Again this is not an argument, but the statement of an experience. It formulates the religious ground for the certainty of an eternal destiny for man. The immediate experience of communion with God implies man's potentiality for participating in the eternal — which God is. The certainty about man's eternal destiny is identical with his communion with God. This is, so to speak, an *argumentum ad hominem*, an existential argument which cannot be transformed into an objective, theoretical one. Nevertheless Jesus does present an argument; he does not require the submission to an authoritative doctrine that his churches later demanded.

The problems raised about man's eternal destiny by the two types of religion are conceptualized in the philosophical inquiry into the problem. Here Plato is the representative figure, but he is not isolated. The origins of his thought are to be found in Orphic mysticism, and he has been adopted by Jewish and Christian theology. In a sense he thus bridges the void between the mystical and the prophetic types.

We must distinguish the motive from the arguments in Plato. The motive is found in *Phaedrus* (249): "For a man, in order to have understanding of universals, . . . must have the recollection of those things which our soul once saw while following God — when, regardless of what we now call beings, she looked towards the true being. And therefore the mind of the philosopher alone has wings." The doctrine of immortality is a description of man's essential nature, which is eternally connected with the true and the good and with Being itself. The eternal element in the soul makes participation in the eternal possible — a possibility which is actualized by the philosopher, who is called "the man who lives in recollection of those things in which God abides." This also is an *argumentum ad hominem*. The certainty of an eternal destiny exists only in the experience in which we are grasped by the true and the good; the "philosopher," in Plato, is the man who is liberated from the common delusions of the "cave" — not the professor of philosophy. In this respect the argument is analogous to that of Jesus.

There are also seemingly objective arguments for immortality in Plato. But they are not real arguments; they are existential experiences, dialectically expressed. Socrates, who pursues them, especially in the dialogue *Phaedon*, says, "You cannot be altogether confident of them." As conclusions they are not valid, but as descriptions of the eternal element in finite man they are valid. They point to the creative independence of the human spirit with respect to the true and the good. This does not prove the existence of an immortal substance, the soul, but it describes man's participation in the eternal.

In these three forms one common idea is expressed: man's essential participation in the eternal. The ways of this participation are different. They shall be described and evaluated presently, but at this point the existence of an eternal destiny for man is in question. The certainty of such a destiny is not dependent on objective arguments; it is implied in immediate, existential experiences and cannot be undermined by theoretical criticisms. Since they are not based on objective arguments, they cannot be refuted by them.

II. The basic symbols of eternal life, their validity and their limits.

All images of eternal life are symbols and not statements about empirical objects or happenings. This is the reason why arguments in the context of empirical knowledge can neither corroborate nor refute them. Their language is a religious language and religious language is always and by necessity symbolic. It takes empirical material and uses the categories of finitude, especially that of time, to express the dimension of the ultimate in being and meaning, but it uses them in such a way that they point beyond themselves. And this "pointing beyond" makes them symbolic.

Symbolic language is valid in the sense that it is the only possible language for expressing the experience of man's participation in the eternal. Nor are the symbols by any means arbitrary. They are authentic when they are born out of a genuine participation and they are adequate if they express the experience correctly and graphically.

There is a basic polarity of all life which can be called individualization and participation. Everything stands under this polarity, and its tension derives from the fact that the more individualized a being is, the more it is able to participate. In man we have complete individualization and universal participation. The symbols of eternal life may be distinguished basically according to the predominance of the elements of individualization or participation. If the participation in the eternal is symbolized by envisioning the finite individual completely drawn back into the Ground of all Being, we can speak of "symbols of proceeding from and receding into the One." With the opposite approach we can speak of "symbols of being created by and reunited with the Ground of Being." The former belongs to the mystical type, the latter to the prophetic type. Each of them, however, appears in three different ways. The proceeding of the finite from the infinite and its receding into it can be imagined in mystical, naturalistic or idealistic symbolism. The being created and reunited can be imagined in the symbols of the immortality of the soul, of the resurrection of the body, or of the participation in the Kingdom of God.

The symbol of eternal life in terms of the proceeding of the individual from and its receding into the Ground of its being is given its most monumental and historically effective expression in the return of the individual Atman to the universal Brahman. The world, including the gods (who are not more but less immortal than the ascetics) is a product of a breath of Brahma, to be recalled after a certain time, or the world is a deception created by the maya, to be dissolved by the ascetic. The Nirvana as a symbol of eternal life indicates the life of absolute fullness, not the death of absolute nothingness. The life of Nirvana is beyond all distinction of subject and object; it is everything because it is nothing definite.

As in all symbols of eternal life, the image of the future grows out of an experience of the present. The eternal is now present in him who has reached the state which the Japanese Zen calls the formless self beyond subject and object. But in order to reach this, many reincarnations are necessary.

They are continuations of temporal existence and consist of punishment and suffering. Only the end of temporal existence brings full participation in eternal life. In it individualization is transcended by participation. A full recession to the "Ground" has taken place. But, we may ask critically, how can the One be abundance if there is no differentiation within it? And what does reincarnation of the same subject mean, if there is no awareness of the identity of the subjects in each reincarnation?

The second form in which the symbols of eternal life describe the individual as proceeding from and receding into the Ground of Being identifies the Ground to which the individual life returns with the life of the universe. It is the naturalistic in contrast to the mystical form of the symbolism of eternal life. There are many forms of naturalism where it is obvious that symbols of eternal life are used. One thinks of the Stoics and their doctrine of the participation of the wise men in the universal logos, or people like Giordano Bruno or Goethe and their cosmic enthusiasm, or of Spinoza and his love for the eternal substance, or of Nietzsche and his ecstatic concept of life affirming itself in eternal return. This type of naturalism emphasizes the coming from and returning to the universal life which for it represents life eternal. Participation in the ecstatically experienced universe conquers the anxiety arising from man's finite state. Many people have lived and died like Spinoza with this feeling. A less obviously symbolic naturalism appears in its mechanistic type, usually called materialism. The element of relinquishing the demand for an eternal significance of the individual as individual is especially strong in it. Yet one often feels that it is a serene, even a superior resignation. This is possible because in the knowledge and intuition of natural processes, the materialist identifies himself with the essential nature of things and by such identification conquers his anxiety.

But while in this type of naturalism we often find noble resignation, we also often find a cynical overcompensation for hidden despair which appropriates the naturalistic perspective in order to give the thinker's personal cynicism a philosophical validity, which is just the opposite of noble resignation. The proponents of materialism, however, are not aware of the fact that their thought, as well as the superior resignation to which it gives rise, expresses a dimension of reality which is unintelligible by any theory of universal mechanism. With all its assertions — indeed, in its very resignation — naturalism witnesses to the eternal dignity of man.

The third form of the symbols of eternal life in which individualization is subdued by participation is the idealistic one. It is more directly dependent on the mystical form and shows mystical elements whenever it appears. But it is a conceptualized mysticism. The struggle in which it first was formulated was directed against Plato's attempt to unite individuality and participation. Its first great representative, Aristotle, criticized Plato's concept of the immortal soul insofar as it is the individual soul.

For Aristotle, only the universal mind is eternal; and it is eternal insofar as it participates in God's eternal self-intuition.

A similar idea was developed by the Arabian philosopher, Averroes, in the 12th century. He followed Aristotle in dissolving the eternity of the individual in the eternity of the consciousness of the human race. Eternal, for him, is the universal creative Mind, not the creative individual. In Hegel it is the eternal Spirit which alone possesses eternity. Eternal life is participation in the creative actualization of the eternal Spirit, which happens in the processes of nature and history. Participation in them through culture and religion is participation in eternal life.

As the idealistic types of symbolization of eternal life were attacked before Hegel, so was he attacked from the theological side because of the lack of a doctrine of immortality in idealism. These attacks were reactions of the individual pole against the pole of participation in the understanding of eternity. Kierkegaard's passionate criticism of Hegel was made in the name of the individual, deciding, despairing and faithful self and its eternal destiny. In spite of the low standing of idealism today (for it has become disreputable to be called an idealist), the idea of an eternal participation of the creative mind of the individual in the universal Mind has considerable weight among humanists, and is also entertained by several religious thinkers. A critical evaluation of this type points to the fact that the spirit is creative only as a union of the rational and the vital (which includes the unconscious, the bodily and the social). For it is in the body that the principle of individualization is realized. A universe of mental functions is not "eternal life." The eternal self-intuition of the pure mind in Aristotle is not life. Hegel reaches down to life and history, but the eternal process is the dialectical play of logical forms and not eternal life. This is the limit of the idealistic form of the principle of the proceeding and receding of the individual in relation to the universal.

The three other forms of a symbolization of eternal life are determined by the preservation of the individual in eternal life. We have called them "symbols of being created and being reunited."

The first one is the doctrine of the immortality of the soul. In its classical form it describes the fall of the soul from the realm of the eternal essences to which it belongs into the realm of existence, matter, temporality, genesis and decay. It also describes the return of the soul to its former state, through a process of individual salvation. The eternal life of the soul which it anticipates in its bodily prison and to which it returns is individual participation in the supratemporal world. Eternal life is intuition of the essences and ultimately of God. The individual is preserved, but only in its reunion with the eternal.

The history of these ideas, their amalgamation with the Christian tradition, their transformation by the philosophers of the Enlightenment into the idea of moral progress after death, their criticism by Hume and Kant, the attempts to restate the idea — all this shows the difficulties immanent in the symbols of immortality. The danger becomes clear in its use in contemporary American Protestantism, especially in secularized Protestantism. There it is understood as a desirable continuation of life after death indefinitely. This popular belief has actually taken precedence over most of the great tenets of Christian thought, including God, sin and salvation, and the concept of eternal life has been replaced by that of an endless temporal life. The "life hereafter" is imagined as a bodiless continuation of the experiences and activities of this life. The classical doctrine of immortality has become a popular Christian superstition. Many factors in our culture have fostered this development. The desire to continue activities which seem important and are cut off by death, the valuation of the individual in his intellectual capacities, the affirmation of life as such, the moralistic undercurrent of American Christianity, the refusal to accept the seriousness of death — all this has contributed to the replacement of the idea of eternal life by the expectation of endless temporal life. There must be added a large amount of sentimentality about death and the desire to remove it from the attention of the living. The result is an interpretation of death which robs it of its crucial character and refuses to contemplate its reality. One continues to live after one has died in almost the same way, but without a body — blessed spirits, walking on beautiful meadows. This has nothing to do with Christianity and very little to do with the classical doctrine. One is not aware of the fact that endless existence would be hell, whatever the content of such life might be. To continue the finite beyond the limits of its finitude is endless punishment and not eternal fulfillment.

The predominance of the individual element in the symbols of eternal life has been most emphatically expressed in the symbol of the resurrection of the body. It is the symbol which, after a history in Parsiism and later Judaism, was accepted by the New Testament authors and all Christian churches. This is partly the cause, partly the result of the belief in the resurrection of the Christ. Its basic motive is the Biblical emphasis on the physical world as divine creation and therefore the emphasis on the unity of body and soul in man. This anti-dualistic bias, especially of the Old Testament, entails a strong affirmation of the total personality as eternally meaningful. And the total personality includes the body in which the individual existence in time and space expresses itself. The contrast between Spirit and flesh, or Spirit and matter, as used in Biblical language, does not refer to different parts of man, but refers to contrasting states of the whole man. Including his body, he is either determined by Spirit or by flesh, either by the divine Presence, or by that which separates from God, the bondage to the finite, not by the finite as such.

This agrees with the idea that the individual human's face is able to express the unique spirit which makes of him an incomparable self. The art of the individual portrait is an acknowledgement of the fact, for which no dualistic thinking can account, that the atoms and cells of the body can express spirit, and are therefore worthy to be remembered beyond the limits of a man's existence in time and space. Neither can dualistic thinking make comprehensible the idea of the sacramental embodiment of the divine Spirit in physical materials like water, wine and oil. In the most universal view, dualism can explain the universe only in terms of a fall of the spirit from itself, not as creation. For as created it is a positive manifestation of the divine Ground and able to participate in eternal life. In some way the symbol of the resurrection is a logical consequence of the symbol of creation. Both presuppose that the forms and structures of the material world are eternally present beyond potentiality and actuality in the divine life.

The difficulties of this symbol are several. It is highly figurative; therefore its distortion when taken literally is especially absurd and dangerous. The medieval pictures of the resurrection of the dead are expressions of a primitive symbolism which was criticized by Paul when he spoke of a spiritual body. He was afraid of the "nakedness" of being a mere spirit, but he was not willing to fall into primitive literalism. We can understand Paul's phrase only as a postulate which limits the symbol by two signposts — spiritual and body — without describing what lies between them.

A second difficulty is the combination of the resurrection of the dead with the "day of consummation and judgment," an equally highly figurative symbolic set of ideas. Whatever they mean, the implication of their connection with the symbol of the resurrection is that the end of the present life, even if it does not last more than one day, decides definitively the eternal destiny of a man. The complete irrationality of such an assertion has produced the idea of a development after death, which may change this destiny. According to the Roman Church, it is Purgatory which produces a slow and painful purification in preparation for the ultimate judgment. But this does not refer to those who without the body of resurrection are waiting for the resurrection either for eternal life or eternal death. In Protestantism, especially under the predominance of moral and educational principles in the theology of the Enlightenment, an intermediate state for further development between death and resurrection was postulated. In some, like Lessing — the greatest representative of the German Enlightenment — it took the form of an almost Indian doctrine of reincarnation. This shows how the same motives drive toward similar solutions, bridging the difference of the types to a certain degree.

We mentioned the concept "eternal death" as the opposite to eternal life. It is significant that in the language of the New Testament there are two symbolic expressions for the condemning judgment: everlasting punishment and eternal death. The first corresponds to everlasting blessedness, the second to eternal life. This language shows the oscillation in New Testament symbolism between an unsublimated and sublimated symbolism. Unsublimated is the symbolization of eternal salvation or condemnation by endless temporality in joy or pain. Literalism in this respect is psychologically absurd, because both joy and pain in the temporal process can only be felt intermittently; but it is also theologically wrong, because in every human being the positive as well as the negative are ambiguously interwoven in his life-process. Therefore, the terms eternal life and eternal death are systematically preferable.

The question, asked most insistently, about the state after death is whether self-consciousness is a quality both of the eternal reunion with the divine life and of the lasting separation from it. To this we must answer that self-consciousness as we experience it in time and space is bound to temporality. Without continually moving and changing perceptions, a state of existence would occur in which the difference between subject and object would disappear. But eternity is not timelessness, and the participation in it is not extinction of the self. As analogy, some ecstatic experiences may be mentioned. The same truth is relevant here as in all our interpretations: you can erect two signposts, but you cannot describe what lies between them. Eternal life is neither continuation nor extinction of the conscious self.

We contrasted eternal life with eternal death. But we must now change the phrase eternal death to give it a precise meaning. Since eternity is the quality of God, death is not eternal, but the negation of eternity. And, like eternal life, this is an experience here and now, namely the threatening loss of the meaning of one's life by separation from its eternal Ground. With the Gospel of John, we must interpret the symbolism of places by the experience in inner states.

A last question is how the different states, distinguished in the symbols of eternal life, are related to each other and to the universe. Here an exclusive emphasis on the individual has produced the doctrine of double predestination to heaven or hell. This doctrine has been implicitly refuted by the analyses previously given. But the question remains, what about the differences, not only between men, but between all beings and parts of the universe? How to solve the riddle of the unequal capacities for the reception of the light coming from the dimension of the eternal? The answer is given in the third of the symbols of creation and reunion, the Kingdom of God. The symbol of the Kingdom of God implies universal fulfillment, a new heaven and a new earth, but not in terms of a receding of the universe into its Ground, but in a reunion of all separated and heterogeneous elements of being in the unity and clarity of the divine life. More than this cannot be said. God will be "all in all," as Paul expresses it. In this ecstatic symbol of fulfillment the contrast of the types is lessened but not completely obliterated. Here a decision cannot be avoided. The Western world, even if it does not use the phrase, has decided for the symbol of the Kingdom of God because in the significance of the individual person the ideas of social justice and the valuation of history are implied. The future history of religion will be largely an encounter of the two central symbols of eternal life: Nirvana and the Kingdom of God. For in these symbols all the fundamentals of the two contrasting experiences of existence are expressed.

Symbols of eternal life are not answers to a particular question; they are answers to the question implied in human existence itself.

SYMPOSIUM SERIES

1. Jurgen Moltman *et al.*, **Religion and Political Society**
2. James Grace, editor, **God, Sex, and the Social Project: The Glassboro Papers on Religion and Human Sexuality**
3. M. Darrol Bryant and Herbert Richardson, editors, **A Time for Consideration: A Scholarly Appraisal of the Unification Church**
4. Donald G. Jones, editor, **Private and Public Ethics: Tensions Between Conscience and Institutional Responsibility**
5. Herbert Richardson, editor, **New Religions and Mental Health: Understanding the Issues**
6. Sheila Greeve Davaney, editor, **Feminism and Process Thought: The Harvard Divinity School/Claremont Center for Process Studies Symposium Papers**
7. International Movement, A.T.D./Fourth World, **Children of Our Time: The Children of the Fourth World**
8. Jenny Hammett, **Woman's Transformations: A Psychological Theology**
9. S. Daniel Breslauer, **A New Jewish Ethics**
10. Darrell J. Fasching, editor, **The Jewish People in Christian Preaching**
11. Henry Vander Goot, **Interpreting the Bible in Theology and the Church**
12. Everett Ferguson, **Demonology of the Early Christian World**
13. Marcia Sachs Littell, editor, **Holocaust Education: A Resource Book for Teachers and Professional Leaders**
14. Char Miller, editor, **Missions and Missionaries in the Pacific**
15. John S. Peale, **Biblical History as the Quest for Maturity**
16. Joseph A. Buijs, editor, **Christian Marriage Today: Growth or Breakdown ?**
17. Michael Oppenheim, **What Does Revelation Mean for the Modern Jew?**
18. Carl F. H. Henry, **Conversations with Carl Henry: Christianity for Today**
19. John T. Biermans, **The Odyssey of New Religious Movements: Persecution, Struggle, Legitimation; A Case Study of the Unification Church**
20. Eugene Kaellis, **Toward a Jewish America**
21. Andrew Wilson, editor, **How Can the Religions of the World be Unified?: Interdisciplinary Essays in Honor of David S.C. Kim**
22. Marcia Sachs Littell, **The Holocaust Forty Years After**
23. Ian H. Angus, **George Grant's Platonic Rejoinder to Heidegger: Contemporary Political Philosophy and the Question of Technology**
24. George E. Clarkson, **Grounds for Belief in Life After Death**, and Paul Tillich, **"Symbols of Eternal Life"**
25. Herbert Richardson, editor, **On the Problem of Surrogate Parenthood: Analyzing the Baby M Case**

GENERAL THEOLOGICAL SEMINARY
NEW YORK